Adopting Solo

Sarah Fisher

Copyright © 2016 by Sarah Fisher
All rights reserved. No part of this publication may be reproduced, distributed or transmitted in any form or by any means, without prior written permission.

Author's Note

To protect those involved, names have been changed throughout the book. This story is based on real events but some timings and identifying details have been changed.

Acknowledgements

To my son for being the wonderful little boy he is. Thank you for all you have taught and given me.

To my parents for always being there. For learning how I parent and supporting me every step of the way.

To my brother for your unwavering support, babysitting services and understanding.

To all my friends who have stood by my side through the ups and the downs.

To Mrs B, Mr J and Mrs F for picking me up when I needed it. I don't know if we'd have gotten through without your knowledge and understanding. Thank you to all the teachers who have taken the time to understand trauma and attachment, and the impact it has.

To Michelle Shapiro and Dr Peter Jakobs for showing me a way of parenting that brought more peace and harmony to our house.

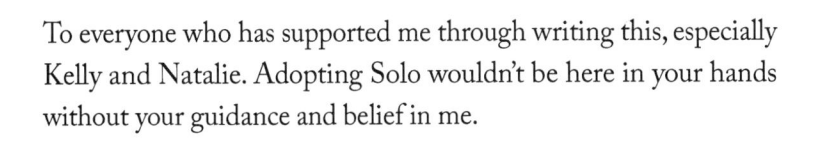

To everyone who has supported me through writing this, especially Kelly and Natalie. Adopting Solo wouldn't be here in your hands without your guidance and belief in me.

To my wonderful editor Kris Emery for sticking with me as Adopting Solo took shape.

To all those I've met on Twitter, Facebook and in the Single Adopters Network. Your unfailing support for everyone is amazing.

Table of Contents

Foreword	ix
Part 1 — Meeting Munchkin... AKA Introductions	1
Part 2 — Munchkin Moves In	28
Part 3 — Meltdowns, Milestones and Many a New Experience	36
Part 4 — Seeking Our Supporters	57
Part 5 — Summer Holiday Success!	84
Part 6 — Settling Into a New Normal	94
About The Author	143

Foreword

Growing up, I loved looking after children. I always thought I'd have a child by birth. In my 20s, I was sure I would, although I thought about adopting too. Since I didn't want to be an 'old mum', I suppose I thought of adopting as a fall-back position. I made the decision to adopt if I hadn't had children by the time I was 35, but I didn't share that decision with anyone else.

As I moved into my 30s, I had a job in a school, which I loved. I was helping children get the best start in life. I wasn't in the classroom but I was having an impact on their lives nonetheless. It felt good and I threw myself into it, working long hours and giving it all I had. Sometimes more.

I made myself ill with stress. Despite knowing in my heart that I wanted children, I'd identified as a career girl by then. I kept going and going, telling myself and others that I didn't want kids. My weekends often involved spending the whole time in my PJs eating junk food and watching re-runs of The West Wing. I loved my lifestyle, complete freedom to do what I wanted when I wanted. I travelled, always south to somewhere warm! I saw friends and enjoyed myself. I remember it mostly as a wonderful time.

Sarah Fisher

Something was missing though. And as I turned 35, I went back to thinking about adopting.

As I reflected, I returned to the idea that there were and are so many children needing a loving family. Adopting felt like a good thing to do, something I wanted to do. I'd always been aware of how many children don't get the start in life that I did. I was fortunate to travel to Kosovo on three separate occasions to work with children there after the Kosovo War. It was an eye-opening, heart-breaking experience that taught me so much and ignited my passion to enhance children's early years the best I could. And this flame continued to burn within me.

Nine months after my 35th birthday, I contacted Social Services and registered my interest in adopting a child. That was the start of my adoption journey. Since that day, my life has completely changed. At times, it has felt like it changed for the harder. Much harder! And yet, it is totally and utterly worthwhile. The best decision I've ever made.

Looking back, I wonder if my thoughts of adopting in the early days might even have stopped me having birth children. Was it a subconscious decision to not find the 'right' man and settle down? Maybe the desire to adopt was always there; I just wasn't ready to act on it earlier or deal with the trials and tribulations of being an adoptive mum.

However I look at it, one thing is certain. I'm just a mum just like any other. Yes, it's through adoption, but I'm a mum first and foremost.

Adopting Solo

Further down the road of our adoption journey, I now have a wonderful son who makes me so proud. I love seeing how he grows every day (although if he could stop physically growing for a bit that would be great!) and being the person who gets to give him the best start in life I can. How he became my son is irrelevant. He is my son and always will be.

I wrote Adopting Solo to help others see the beauty of being a single adopter and showing you it can be done.

Throughout this book, my hope for you is that you recognise your own adoption journey in my story, see and understand the difficulties others have too, and find words of encouragement and hope. It hasn't always been an easy road, but I am proof that it's worth it.

Adopting solo is possible. Adopting Solo shows you why.

Now you know how I came to adopt, here's our story.

Part 1
Meeting Munchkin... AKA Introductions

DAY 1

Meeting my son for the first time melted my heart like never before. I'd seen photos and been given lots of information about him, but meeting him was something else. It's like when you read a book about someone and then get to meet them in person. It brought everything to life.

I remember driving to where he lived back then. It was an early start followed by two-and-a-half hours of nerves and excitement all mixed together. Worries and questions filled my head... *What if he doesn't like me? What if I don't like him? What if I've made a mistake? Can I really do this?*

I'd arranged to meet my social worker, Mary, just round the corner from his house a little before we were due to be there. This gave me a bit of breathing space. With both of us sitting in my car, Mary reassured me it was going to be okay, then reminded me of how it would unfold. She mentioned I should be careful with my emotions in front of the child too, for instance, going into another room if I felt like crying. I thought that was a bit odd at first, but Mary explained gently that he might think I didn't like him or he'd done something wrong if he saw me crying. A happy poker face was going to be needed, so that my son-to-be didn't see any doubt in my eyes.

Just 15 minutes later, we parked up outside the foster carers' home and knocked on the door. That's the moment I think I stopped breathing! The door opened. There stood his foster mum and, as I peered past her shoulder, the little boy who would become my son. I fell in love with him right there on the doorstep. He was tiny, cute, just adorable. He looked so much younger than his age and I was taken aback by how small he was. The photo I'd seen of him made him look taller. I went inside and said hello. When he replied, 'Hello Mummy', my heart fluttered. He took me straight into the living room because he wanted to show me a beautiful photobook that his school had made him as a leaving present. We looked through all the pictures and read all the notes from staff and children. It was such a thoughtful gift. Sitting together on the sofa, that was it – our first few moments together.

That first hour together was lovely. We talked and we played. He was keen to show me his room and his toys. The foster carers had started packing up his stuff ready to come to mine. I was surprised at how much physical stuff he had. They'd done a brilliant job of keeping everything over the long stretch of time he had been with these carers.

It all felt surprisingly natural and in some ways like I'd known my little Munchkin forever. (That's his name for the sake of this book. Throughout the rest of *Adopting Solo*, I'll continue to refer to my son as Munchkin.)

After we'd seen his room and his toys, Munchkin wanted to go through the photo album I'd done for him and watch the video I'd made with Mary. She had videoed me on my iPad as I walked round showing my house to Munchkin. I was anxious doing it. *Was I showing him the right things? Was I coming across as a nice mummy? What if he saw it and hated me?* All of those questions and more. It was surreal making that recording. I made the arguably regrettable mistake of saying he could come into my room when he woke up in the morning. (With hindsight, I *really* should have checked how early he woke up before saying that!) The album had more photos of the house, as well as the local park and my family, including my cats. Both the album and video had been given to him on the day his social worker Emily told him she'd found a mummy for him. He even took the album to school he was so proud of it. How adorable is that? He still looks at it now.

Emily had told Munchkin about me a week after the matching panel had taken place and we'd received written agreement. The matching panel is a group made up of people who usually either work or are involved in adoption in some way. Often, they don't know the child personally, just from the paperwork they receive. They decide whether or not you'll make a good parent to that particular child. It's a bit like a job interview, with a panel of 10 people firing questions at you from all angles, about a complete range of topics in no particular order. To say I was terrified would be an understatement, but thankfully they agreed with the match.

And so we were united. After about an hour at the house getting to know my son-to-be, Munchkin's social worker turned up with her manager to confirm the plan for Introductions (the period when you get to know each other, before the child moves in with you). Emily and her manager checked how the first meeting had gone, and while our meeting was going on in the dining room, Munchkin was sent into the playroom, where he could see us through the glass but not hear anything. I could tell he wasn't happy about it! Yet my focus was on the meeting. I was asked if I was okay and whether wanted to continue with the adoption. Some people walk away at this point, when they realise they can't do it. How heart-breaking that must be for everyone involved, especially the child, who is effectively being abandoned. I knew there was no way I was walking away. I said so.

We agreed the plan for the rest of Introductions and I spent another few hours playing with Munchkin before leaving just after lunch. That first trip home I filled my car with his belongings, but by no means all of them!

Since that meeting, Munchkin has asked me what it was about and why he wasn't allowed to join us. The conversation went like this:

> **Munchkin:** Mummy, what was that meeting you had when I wasn't allowed to come?
>
> **Me:** Which meeting are you talking about, sweetie?
>
> **Munchkin:** The one at my foster carers' house, when I had to stay in the playroom whilst all the adults talked.
>
> **Me:** Ah, that was to check I hadn't run away screaming.
>
> **Munchkin:** Really?
>
> **Me:** And that you hadn't either.

I had him in fits of giggles at that answer and that meeting is now known as the 'run away screaming meeting'. It does come up randomly in conversation, so that's how I tackle it, telling him effectively what it was, but also making him laugh.

I drove home in a daze and unloaded the car thinking, 'Wow, I'm going to be a mum'. I was exhausted that evening and crashed into bed before another early start the following day, when I'd be heading back to meet him again.

Finally, it was feeling real.

DAY 2

Another early start. I left at 6.30am and headed to the foster carers' home for the second day running. Munchkin, his foster mum and I spent the day together playing and getting to know each other. We went to the park in the afternoon. Along the way, I had a great opportunity to find out more about Munchkin from the foster carer's perspective, as the little one scootered off ahead. I asked her what he liked and disliked, how her and her partner parented him, what the rules were in her house, and what Munchkin's general behaviour was like. I knew that would probably be different when he moved in with me, but it was good to get a basic understanding. Back at the house, we spent time packing some more of his stuff before I left. Excitedly, he told me about all the toys he had and games he played.

That day is a bit of a blur. Being in someone else's house while I started parenting my child felt odd at times, especially with his familiar carer still right there. Taking over that role during Introductions isn't easy, particularly when you know you want to do it slightly differently. And yet, his foster carers were lovely, so supportive. They offered advice, but understood that it was only natural I'd want to do it my own way.

We finished the day by having dinner together. I put Munchkin to bed for the first time, which was a totally new experience for me. I'd never gotten a child ready for bed before. The nearest I'd ever been was babysitting, but the children were always in their PJs ready to go. It was just a case of putting them in the actual bed. Despite my inexperience, Munchkin got ready for bed perfectly happily and didn't seem to mind me being there, although he was understandably shy. We did story time and I tucked him in. Like me, he must have been exhausted, because he fell asleep quickly. My new son looked angelic cuddled under the duvet; being the one to put him to bed felt so special.

Back downstairs, I spent time talking to the foster carers and asking the questions I couldn't ask in front of Munchkin. Questions about his behaviour; how he interacted with others, both adults and children; if there were any issues I needed to know about that I didn't already; how they thought he was coping with meeting me. Their support during Introductions was invaluable and I felt lucky to have such caring people helping me through the process.

That night, I stayed in a local hotel. Totally shattered, I honestly don't think I'd have managed the drive home! Although there was one more job to do before hitting my bed. The hotel was next to a massive Ikea store, which was wonderful since I'd realised I needed yet *more* storage. In a sleepy haze, I walked round and bought a selection of storage items including a toy box. I think I was just picking up anything that might do the job as I didn't have the brain power to think properly about what I needed! (And who doesn't love a wander round Ikea? That and the John Lewis over the road, I was one happy lady. John Lewis would have to wait for another day though.)

Despite the exhaustion from the day, I struggled to get to sleep that night, with so many emotions going round and round in my head. It was impossible to switch off my brain.

DAY 3

The following morning, I was up early and at the foster carers in time for breakfast to eat with Munchkin. I remember creeping in and finding him cuddled up on the sofa watching TV. He was so engrossed in it that it took me a few moments to get him to register I was there. Curled up in his PJs, he was endearing, even more so for his small size. He looked several years younger than he was.

After breakfast, Munchkin got dressed and we decided to go out together for the day, just the two of us. I was certainly nervous and I think he was too. It was a long time since I'd driven a car with a child in the back. We set off for a nearby zoo and arrived with no problems. Munchkin had been there before, which must have helped him feel safer and more secure. I was overly cautious about him getting out of the car in the carpark and making sure he stuck to my side at all times, as I was terrified of him being hit by a car. We joined the queue for tickets and, to the rest of the world, we just looked just like any normal mum and child on a day out at the zoo. All of those emotions I was feeling, and no doubt all of my son's emotions too, we hid them well. If only they knew…

That day was a great opportunity for us to get to know each other better. We spent several hours walking around looking at the animals. (Although, as far as my son was concerned, the very average play area was clearly as interesting as the main attraction!) We had fun that day and I took lots of photos to keep as a memory of our first outing. And gosh, he does like to pose when the camera appears! I remember asking him constantly if he needed the toilet, was thirsty or hungry. I must have sounded a bit over-the-top, but I was worried I'd miss something and he'd be too afraid to ask. As it happened, he was fine. Although we did eat a lot of chips and ice cream. All in a good cause!

By mid-afternoon, we were ready to go back to the foster carers' home. When we returned, we told them all about the day. I felt like I could relax a little and had achieved a new milestone – I'd managed to take him out for the day and not lose him!

Until dinner was ready, we spent the afternoon playing and helping his foster mum prepare for his leaving party the next day. It was a good insight into a child's party and also the tastes Munchkin had for food and so on. Putting so many party bags together and trying to stop a child eating the sweets or playing with the toys was quite a juggling act! Luckily, though, meals seemed to be fine. I noticed he sat down happily and ate with no fuss. With each and every thing we did, I was learning more about him and making a mental note. He had a good appetite and ate a wide variety of food, loving lots of vegetables, which surprised me. One of his favourite vegetables is cauliflower and he loves sprouts, though I'm fond of neither. He evens prefers potatoes to chips. (If only I was the same!)

After dinner, Munchkin's bedtime routine started quickly. His foster carer told me how early he woke up, which was why he had to go to bed early. I could barely believe he got up at 5.30am most days. Maybe I just didn't want to… But I would soon learn it was true when he moved in! I did his bedtime routine again that night, read to him, and tucked him up. The second time, it still felt slightly strange, but I realised I would be doing this every night for years to come.

That night, I drove home with yet another car load of Munchkin things. I was tired emotionally and physically. It had been an incredible few days that are imprinted on my mind forever. All the apprehension of meeting Munchkin and uncertainty of what would happen was exhausting. Yet at the same time, I felt overjoyed at meeting him and becoming his mum. Such a mix of emotions went through me on that car journey home to my house, made all the stranger by having so much of Munchkin's past in the boot of the car and back seat. Items from his birth family and his life with his foster carers filled my car. It was hard to cope with that connection at times, and this was one of those times, though I knew its vital importance to my son.

DAY 4

The next day was Mothering Sunday and I had the day off. By 'off', I mean I wasn't seeing Munchkin that day. His foster family had organised a big farewell party for him (and I do mean big!) but we'd all agreed I wouldn't be there, so that Munchkin could focus on spending time with friends for the last time. From the photos I saw, his carers had gone to a lot of effort. It looked like an enjoyable time with games and people of all ages who had been part of his life while he'd lived with his foster parents. My son had remained with the same foster family during his whole time in care (nearly four years) so had developed strong bonds with them. He had many friends locally from school and Beavers, so this party was important for lots of people, not just him. We were eating the cake for the rest of the week it was so big!

Although it was strange not seeing him that day, it was also kind of nice. I was exhausted, emotionally and physically. A day to relax was what I needed, particularly knowing how full on it would be from the following day onwards.

Lying in bed that morning it started to sink in that I was becoming a mum. Having finished work the night before Introductions started, I hadn't had the time to stop and think about it. Before meeting my son, it had all felt a bit intangible. I'd been working flat out. Weekends were spent getting the house ready, buying what I needed and preparing his room. I hadn't given myself any space to think about the reality of it coming true. Maybe that was self-preservation; keeping busy, my subconscious not allowing me to think about it too much, not wanting to worry about whether I could do it, whether I'd taken the right path. I knew in my heart (and my gut) that this was the course I should be taking. That was my overriding feeling. The worries? Well, they were definitely there. Still today, I wonder if I'm parenting well enough. The difference is now I'm sure that's a normal worry for any parent to have. (At least that's what I keep telling myself!)

I spent most of that last day of freedom relaxing at home, stretched out on the sofa watching Sunday TV. My wonderful brother took me out for a Mother's Day lunch. After all, I was a mum now, or near enough. It was a restful day. And looking back, I realise how much I needed that time and space to let my head sort itself out a bit.

That evening, as I was packing for the following night away, one of my cats took umbrage at me leaving again and sat in the suitcase. I will never forget the look on her face, clearly unhappy at my plans. Every time I tried to put something in the case or remove her, she took a swipe at me. I wondered how she would cope when the house became busier and noisier courtesy of a seven-year-old, since she was one for hiding away if people came round. I'm sure that she sensed things were changing. It wasn't just her I was thinking about though. I was also curious about how things would change and how I would cope. It was just starting to dawn on me how different life was going to be. I don't think it's possible to truly understand until you're living it. The cat is only just finally getting used to having a child around and allowing Munchkin to stroke her, two years later.

DAY 5

I was up at the crack of dawn even though I didn't need to be. And it's unlike me to wake up early if I don't need to.

That morning, Munchkin was coming to me for a visit, just for the day. Emily and his foster mum were bringing him up and they were due about 11am, so I had time to clean the house... and generally panic. The nerves were rising. *What if he didn't like the house? What if he didn't like his room?* I live on the edge of a town with fields and countryside in view. My son was coming from the middle of a big city. It would be a complete change for him on top of everything else. *What if he didn't like it? What if, what if, what if...?* I went on and on. It's surprising how much you can wind yourself up in such a short space of time! I'm sure I'm not the only one whose nerves were frayed.

When they all arrived, I went outside to greet everyone. Munchkin got out of the car and came over to give me a big hug and I remember feeling my heart melt. (It melted a lot in those early days.) We went inside and he went straight up to his room. He knew exactly where it was and the layout of the house from the video I'd sent him. He had apparently been watching it a lot, which of course I hoped was a good thing. He came running back downstairs to get his foster carer and took her upstairs to show her the room too. I'd put some toys and games in there, which thankfully he seemed to like, and gifts from my friends. Having his own room was a big deal for him, especially because he often shared his room at the foster carers' place. His new room would also be much bigger.

At this point, I offered the foster carer and social worker tea and coffee, before realising I don't use milk, so I was a bit stuck! I ran next door and borrowed some coffee and milk. Despite the hiccough, my nerves were starting to settle. And after about an hour, they both left.

Reality set in.

I was a mum. I was responsible for a child.

It was lunchtime, so that gave us something to do together and helped calm me. I'd made sure I had something to eat that he liked and we sat at the table to tuck in. It went well! Task one successfully completed. I could at least feed him!

The rest of that day is blurry in my memory. I know we stayed at home. Beyond that, I can't remember, such was my state of mind. The social workers had all told me to keep it simple and let him get used to the house. At dinner that evening, again I played it safe with something I knew he would like and more importantly I could cook. I'm a vegetarian. (Well, technically a pescatarian as I'm often reminded.) I've eaten that way for years, so as a result, have hardly ever cooked meat. It was a daunting prospect, but since I never expected Munchkin to give up meat, I cooked two dishes at mealtime. (Add in feeding the cats and mealtimes get a bit busy. Particularly as the animals would rather eat our meals than theirs!)

After dinner, Munchkin had a shower and got ready for bed before we drove back down to his foster carers' home. It was a long drive after a long day and emotionally draining for both of us. It was also the first time I'd driven on the motorway with a child in the car, which is a lot more distracting that you realise. I was used to driving along listening to the radio, but instead spent the two-and-a-half hours talking to a child and listening to him sing full blast. It was during that drive that I understood why people *really* have those 'princess on board' signs in their cars!

When we reached his foster home, Munchkin said a quick goodnight before going straight to bed. He usually went to bed at 6.30pm and it was gone 8pm. He was shattered, although fighting it hard. I caught up with his carers, agreed a plan for the following morning, then went to my hotel to collapse myself.

DAY 6

When I returned to the foster carers' for breakfast the next morning, I let myself in to find Munchkin in his PJs on the sofa, again engrossed in the programme. He didn't respond when I said hello and immediately I worried that something was wrong. I sat next to him and started to watch the TV too. He curled up with me, which I took as a good sign. Now I know him better, I believe he was simply too engaged in the television to say anything that day, because he's just the same now. Sometimes it takes several tries to get a response.

After breakfast that morning, we were due to have a midway review. Another of the 'run away screaming meetings' as we now call them. I was asked how I felt, but no-one seemed to want to talk to Munchkin about how he felt at this point. This, I found quite odd. I'm sure his foster carer would have spoken to him, but I was surprised his social worker didn't check how he felt. The meeting didn't last long, and it was deemed to be going well, so we carried on with the programme for the rest of the week.

After the meeting, we played some more and had lunch. Munchkin is a lover of food. I really don't know where he puts it all. His appetite is amazing to me. After eating, the two of us went off to the local park. I wasn't 100% sure where I was going, so I relied on Munchkin a bit. He was on his scooter. And boy, was he fast! It was the first time we'd been out where he wasn't next to me the whole time and that was a nerve-wracking experience. En route to the park, we went past a cornershop. Like many children, he suddenly had to have a drink or else he might die from thirst. Amused at his theory and rather impressed with his acting, I agreed. Once inside, his real motive became obvious, and I couldn't believe I hadn't registered it. Sweets! That was what he really wanted. Apparently they cure thirst – who knew?! After a bit of negotiation (which I'm pretty sure I lost), Munchkin got a drink and a packet of sweets and we were back on our way. Once we got to the playground, we had a good time. I even remembered to take some photos, which I'm so glad I did. They are a wonderful reminder of how much he has changed. We spent ages in the park before heading home, and everything had been going well. Munchkin was doing pretty much as I asked. I got lulled into a false sense of security...

On the journey back, Munchkin started getting resistant. First, he said he wanted to go back to the park instead of going home. To be honest, I wasn't completely sure how to handle it. When we were nearly home, he stopped completely within a hundred yards or so of his old school. He refused to go any further, getting increasingly wound up and cross. He became defiant, stating we were going back to the park, but I stood my ground. I told him no, trying to explain calmly that we weren't. He got worse. I felt more and more out of my depth, which I'm sure he sensed, my unease and worry consequently making him uneasy and worried himself. I was terrified he would just go back to the park on his scooter on his own and I knew there was no way I'd be able to catch up with him. Talking to him wasn't working, but I didn't know what else to try.

After a standoff – and to this day I don't know how long it lasted or what changed – I managed to get him to scooter home. I gave him a push on his scooter to get him going and we set off again. But the rest of the journey wasn't easy, with him often going too far ahead and purposefully hiding, both of which scared me to death. The thought of going back and telling the foster carers I'd lost him wasn't exactly appealing, let alone *actually* losing him.

By the time we got back to the house, Munchkin was being rude. I knew I couldn't let it go and not address it. I had a word with the foster carer and she suggested I dealt with it, as it would be good for both of us to start building some boundaries about behaviour. I knew the foster carer used 'timeout' so thought I'd try that too. Well, it's safe to say that didn't work. Munchkin refused to stay on the bottom stair and ended up running up to his room. I left him to cool down for five minutes, then went up to talk. I sat on the floor and explained why I hadn't been happy with his behaviour; that I'd been worried. Eventually, he started talking to me again. We had a hug and went back downstairs.

I already knew that timeout didn't work as a technique for improving behaviour. From my training during the approval process two years earlier, I knew it wasn't a good idea. Yet for some reason, in the heat of the moment, it's what I chose to do. Maybe I needed to see for myself that it wasn't a brilliant option. Maybe my knowledge and training simply disappeared from my brain when faced with the situation. I feel that the latter is more likely. That need to feel in control is just under the surface during such a new and uncertain time. Knowing that you're being watched and monitored to ensure you'll be okay as a parent adds to the pressure.

Adopting Solo

The rest of the afternoon went smoothly and we packed up the rest of Munchkin's clothes and toys. He liked to tell me where everything had come from as we were putting the items into boxes, so it wasn't a quick task. That evening, I put Munchkin to bed again, which was starting to feel more natural, and went back to my hotel.

DAY 7

Today was going to be a big day! We would pay a visit to Munchkin's new school and he would be staying over at our home for the first time. I collected him from his foster carers and loaded up the car with the remainder of his stuff. We got back with enough time to unload the car and have (what I thought would be) a quick lunch. Quick lunches were virtually impossible back then, as Munchkin ate so slowly. While a slow mealtime can be good in some ways – more time to talk, family time – it can be frustrating, painful even, if you're in a rush. I learnt quickly to allow plenty of time to eat, because the more I tried to rush him, the slower he became.

Emily arrived just after we had eaten as she was coming with us to the school. At this point, Munchkin decided he wasn't going. It was clear that the nerves had set in – totally understandably, as he was having to deal with so many new people and places. Among his worries was that I didn't have a red front door, a dog or a dad for him. And there was me, hoping two cats might suffice… Apparently not!

After a bit of discussion, I managed to get Munchkin to put on his shoes and leave the house. As I recall, some bribery was involved at this point, but it was worth it for the joy I felt as I got him out the door. Once in the car, we drove off to the school, his social worker following in her car. He hadn't seen the school before, so again, it was all new to him. When we arrived, everything seemed fine until I'd parked the car and went to get out. At this point, Munchkin's fear kicked in and he refused to move. Emily came over to find out what was wrong and try talking to him. That didn't work. Munchkin was determined not to budge. I sent the social worker off ahead of us into the school to let them know we were on our way in. Eventually, I managed to get Munchkin out of the car, although I honestly can't remember how. I do have a recollection of *carrying him* up the road to the front door of the school, where I put him down and he strolled in by himself, me totally out of breath from bringing him up the hill!

The school was fantastic. I was so grateful for how compassionate everyone was in helping Munchkin feel at ease. We met the headteacher, Special Educational Needs Co-ordinator (SENCo), who has responsibility for children that need additional support for whatever reason, and his class teacher. The school had a high percentage of adopted children. I'd chosen it because of its reputation for having good understanding of trauma and attachment, and how those circumstances affect children.

I watched Munchkin relax during the meeting as they asked him questions and we showed them his school books. The school was much smaller than he was used to, which I think he found a bit strange as we were shown around. He was introduced to his new classmates, who all seemed welcoming.

After the school visit, his social worker headed off and we went home via the shops to get something for dinner. We went to a small shop, so that Munchkin wasn't too overwhelmed, which seemed to work well at keeping him relaxed. When we got home, we started sorting out some of the stuff we'd brought up that day, finding places for the many, many presents he'd received at his leaving party. So that he wasn't totally overwhelmed, I put some away and did toy rotations over the next few weeks. Well, until Munchkin decided all of his toys should come out and cover what felt like most of the house! We played together until tea time and then curled up on the sofa to watch TV, before ringing his foster carer to tell her about his day.

Bedtime was an easy process that night. He happily showered and got into his PJs. (If only it had stayed that way!) I read him a story and turned out the light, leaving the landing light on and his door open. I waited outside the room for a few moments before going downstairs to make sure he was okay, and while it took some time for him to fall sleep, at last I heard his snoring and headed downstairs relieved.

And then… I had no idea what to do with myself! I didn't want to make too much noise in case I woke him up, but didn't have the emotional energy to do anything. I decided to watch TV for a bit before heading off to bed myself. And by 'watch TV', I mean watching in 15 minute intervals, and checking on Munchkin every quarter of an hour to make sure he was still okay! He was asleep every time…

DAY 8

Well, the next morning was certainly a wakeup call. Literally. Munchkin got up at 5.30am, which meant I did as well. I don't really do mornings. Certainly not 5.30am. I was used to getting up at 6.30am for work, but I didn't particularly like it. I'm an owl, but it was apparent that my son was a lark. On top of being woken up early, I'd hardly slept. It was the first time I'd ever been responsible for a child all night and I was terrified something would go wrong. During the night, I dreamt up so many disaster scenarios it was crazy. Everything from him stopping breathing to breaking his neck falling out of bed! The more tired I got, the crazier the ideas became. It reached the point where I was checking on him constantly. Each time – and unsurprisingly – he was fine. All new parents go through this, I'm sure, but at 3am, lying in the dark with no-one to reassure you, it's incredibly worrying.

And so it was that at 5.30am we got up and went downstairs to watch more TV. I figured this was okay, because it meant my brain didn't have to start functioning yet, which it was thankful for. After a while, we had breakfast, got dressed, and had the whole day ahead of us, which we were going to spend at home by ourselves.

Munchkin wanted to go and see the local park, so we set off to investigate, him on his much-loved scooter and me trying to keep up behind him! The skate park grabbed his attention first. It was school term time, so the park was virtually deserted, other than a three-year-old boy, who was loving the ramps. We were there for what felt like ages, before seeing the rest of the park and visiting the playground.

It was buying lunch on the way home that I learnt taking Munchkin to a shop was not a particularly easy experience. He wanted to buy everything. In an instant, I understood what all my friends had been saying about why they hated going shopping with their children. Back then, I'd thought they were being over the top, but it's 100% true that children can get items into the trolley without you even noticing. To be fair, I'm sure I did this as a child as well, but it doesn't bother you until it's your wallet being hit!

The afternoon was spent back at home, putting away more toys and clothes he'd brought with him and getting to know each other further. How strange it was to suddenly be the parent of a seven-year-old boy. Not only the parenting takes some getting used to, but learning each other's tastes is huge.

That evening for dinner I thought I'd try spaghetti bolognese. Being veggie, I decided to do it with veggie mince and see what he thought. Let's just say, it didn't go down well.

> **Munchkin:** What's for dinner?
>
> **Me:** Spaghetti bolognese.
>
> **Munchkin:** Oh yum, I love that.
>
> **Me:** That's good.

Five mins later after the first mouthful...

> **Munchkin:** Yuck, that's disgusting. I'm not eating it. Make me something else.

Me: What's wrong with it?

Munchkin: It's disgusting. What have you made it with?

Me: Well, I've used veggie mince. If you don't like it, that's okay. Just eat the pasta first, then I'll get you something else.

Munchkin: Never give me that again. It's horrible. I need something else to eat now.

Me: Eat the pasta and you can have some sausages or ham. Which would you prefer?

Munchkin: They are proper ones, aren't they?

Me: Yes. So, which would you like?

Munchkin: Sausages please.

Success! And I'd confirmed he didn't like veggie mince, although he's happily eaten it a few times since without knowing...

After dinner, we headed back to his foster carers' house for bath and bedtime. We were getting used to the drive by then and it amazed me how much of the journey he knew. He'd memorised different landmarks en route and knew when to expect them. And he loved reading the signposts as we went. Looking back, I feel this was his security blanket. He wanted to know where he was and how to get there, just in case anything happened.

After putting him to bed, I caught up with his foster carers, then headed back to my familiar hotel. I called my social worker Mary that night too. She'd been great at keeping in touch and being available in the evenings, knowing that was the best time for me to talk. Her support and experience was invaluable during this period, helping me feel better about what was happening and knowing it was all normal.

DAY 9

When I arrived at the foster carers' house in the morning, it was immediately obvious something was wrong. Munchkin was distressed and finding everything too much. I tried to talk to him, but we all know that being rational isn't easy when you're angry, even harder when you don't understand what's wrong yourself. His foster mum was understandably upset too. Munchkin had lived there a long time, so I imagine it was both joyful and upsetting to see him move to an adoptive home.

I was due to take Munchkin to mine for two nights this time before bringing him back for a final goodbye on Sunday. We talked about what to do, seeing how distressed he was and both wondering if it was a good idea to stick to the plan. The foster family had said goodbye to Munchkin before leaving for school and work, which I've since thought may have made his demeanour worse. I've wondered about whether he thought the plan was being changed without him being told, which could have worried him.

It was hard seeing Munchkin so upset. This was the first time he'd shown any sense of real distress to me or anyone else during

Introductions. Unsure of what to do, we agreed I should call Social Services for advice. Munchkin's social worker Emily said she would come out with her manager, so while we waited, I spoke to Mary on my side. From all parties, there was clearly concern for him, but also a need to follow procedure. When Emily arrived, she spoke to him alone (for the *first time* during Introductions) and took him for a walk round the block. I think he appreciated someone asking if he was okay. I wasn't part of the conversation so don't know what was said, but something seemed to work in helping him settle down and feel more at ease.

While Munchkin was out, the foster carer and I had a chat with Emily's manager, who was *very clear* that we were to go ahead as planned. I was instructed to bring him back on the Sunday, irrespective of how Munchkin was or how distressed he might be. I remember feeling angry at the time that procedure seemed more important than my son's feelings. Handover was at 9am and it was non-negotiable. It *must* be done this way, irrespective of the potential impact on the child. I made it clear that I would contact them if he was so distressed that I felt unsafe driving, as I wasn't going to endanger us. We agreed on that approach, although she reiterated that I was expected back *no matter what*. I got no further explanation when I asked why that was the procedure, but I didn't push it. I still don't know why it had to happen that way, but I imagine there's research or precedent of some kind.

Either way, agreements in place, we left for home. We had a journey that seemed to take an eternity, me still worried, him still wobbly. He would swap from being silent to distractingly noisy. Thankfully, the rest of the day passed fine, as we spent time playing and watching TV. Even bedtime went well, although it did take time to arrange all the teddy bears and figure out which ones would sleep on the bed. It's a highly important decision, you know.

Day 10

The day after is hazy in my mind. I only remember that it started hideously early, something silly again like 5.30am, when Munchkin was wide awake and I most certainly was not! My brain simply will not function at that time of day, and definitely not on a Saturday. We stayed home that day, more playing and getting to know each other. We'd been shopping earlier that week, so we had food in that he liked. I was comforted that this meant one less thing to worry about in an already tricky time. This was the day I decided that Saturday night would be movie night, which meant dinner in front of the TV, popcorn and sweets, while we watched a film together. (Because we all know that you can't watch a film without eating popcorn.) It would become our new family tradition.

I wanted mealtimes to be consistent, so that they formed part of our routine and Munchkin would know when he was eating. This seemed to work well at the start. Slowly over time, it's something that has become less routine and more dependent on our day or how hungry he is. Sometimes he eats ridiculous amounts. Other days he hardly eats anything.

When our film finished, it was bath and bedtime. I still felt a little unsure about how much to help him or leave him to get on with it. He could be very capable for a seven-year-old and I knew he showered by himself at the foster carers'. Yet instinctively, I wanted to look after him and do more. While he was capable of being independent, he had lost out on so much; I wanted to fill those gaps and give him back some of the nurturing he'd missed. For that reason, we started a nightly routine of reading together once he was tucked up in bed. I enjoyed this time together and believe he did too. He asked me to sit under the duvet with him, which gave us some cuddle time. Reading together regularly, I have watched his ability and confidence grow, as well as it helping us bond.

By this time of Introductions, I was exhausted. That night, I collapsed on the sofa after Munchkin was asleep. Although I wanted to sleep, I still couldn't get my head around going to bed at that time, despite knowing it would be another stupidly early morning the next day.

Day 11

And it was! After another 5.30am start, we spent a few hours playing, unpacking, and opening some more of his leaving presents. Although the morning was lovely, it was Sunday and I was beginning to dread taking him back to the foster carers that afternoon, given how he'd been when we'd left two days earlier. I wondered if he could pick up on my worry around how he was going to react. After lunch and packing an overnight bag each for the last time, we headed back to the foster carers. Munchkin was upset and anxious, but was somehow managing to hold it all together. My heart went out to him; it must have been so hard. He'd spent the week to-ing and fro-ing, which would have been unsettling for him. And on top of that, it was now time to go and say goodbye to the family and life he knew.

As an adult, walking away and leaving everything and everyone you know would be painful and frightening. I can't imagine how scared and anxious a child – my son – must have felt.

We arrived at the house and went straight in. After the way it had gone on the Friday when we'd left, I think they were just glad to see us. I stayed awhile and then left, agreeing he would ring me before bedtime and making sure Munchkin knew I'd be back the next day to collect him. He'd been able to choose what they had for dinner and I think the idea of having Chinese takeaway was helping to allay his worries!

That afternoon I spent shopping in the mall next to my hotel. It was wonderful having those last few hours to myself. I treated myself to a big purple towelling dressing gown with a hood. It was in the sale and only available in extra-large, but I got it anyway. I'd wanted one for ages and decided I deserved it. It's so big that it fits both of us – great for cuddles! I bought a few other bits and pieces, then headed back to the car only to find a warden writing me a parking ticket! Despite begging for mercy, he told me he had to issue it, but suggested I write with my mitigating circumstances because I might be let off. (Thankfully, I was and I've learnt my lesson – don't assume Sunday parking is free!)

Back at the hotel, I treated myself to a nice meal in the restaurant and a glass or two of wine. After all I was celebrating. The next day I would be taking my son home for good.

Part 2
Munchkin Moves In

Day 12

I woke early, after a bad night's sleep. The mix of emotions had got the better of me and stopped me from switching off. Instead, my mind had gone through so many different ifs and buts, I had scared myself.

I got up and headed to the foster carers' home for just before 9am. It all felt a bit surreal. In a daze, I kept having to pinch myself to check it was real. I was taking my son home for good. *I was taking my son home for good.* Finally! After a two-year process. It was *actually* happening. I was becoming a mum.

Even though the process had been relatively quick for me, with many adopters waiting much longer, it had still seemed like such a long time. It can feel like life is on hold in a way, because you never know when you might find a match.

Stupidly, I got caught by a speed camera that morning on the way to get him. In some ways, getting caught was good. The flash of the light made me more alert and (as I'm constantly reminded of by Munchkin, if I stray over) driving within the speed limit is clearly the better option.

Adopting Solo

The handover was exceptionally formal and had to be done in a particular way. I was told to wait outside the foster carers' home in my car. I was not allowed into the house. A few minutes later, Emily arrived and came over to check I was alright. Other than feeling sick with a mixture of nerves, excitement and exhaustion, I was fine. (I'm not sure what she would have done if I hadn't been okay!) She went inside to collect my son. A few minutes later, they both came out and she handed him over to me – literally – like a piece of shopping or something. Munchkin's foster carer was under instruction to stay inside, just like I'd had to remain in the car. I found the whole episode completely odd, given the way we had all interacted during Introductions, but I assume there's good reason for doing the handover like this. I never found out.

Munchkin seemed okay, if a little quiet to start. How overwhelming it must have been for him, I thought, and yet the drive home was fine. Munchkin became more and more talkative as the journey progressed, which became the norm for us, reading out the road signs and pointing at the landmarks along the way.

We arrived back home and it was all going well. We were getting on. I was trying hard to relax into the role of Mum and he seemed happy enough. I managed to cook meals he liked, played games he enjoyed, watched TV with him and attempted to chill out. Having someone I didn't know well in my house – who I was now the parent of – did feel a little strange though.

Although the day had gone well, our lifestyle would be different to that at his foster carers; I knew the change would be hard for him on top of everything else. I had created a timetable for our days so that Munchkin knew when mealtimes, bath and bedtimes were. (It even included the cats' mealtimes!) I'd done this to alleviate any worry for him and create structure, but I also wanted to show him the clear differences between his life at the foster carers' and life now we were a family.

Day 13

The second day of living together was as good as the first. I can't say I was used to the early mornings yet. In fact, I felt like I needed a powernap in the afternoon, but I figured I'd get used to it. We spent the morning in our PJs and went to the park in the afternoon at Munchkin's request. The advice from the social workers is to not do anything at all for the first two weeks, just stay at home, not meeting anyone, not seeing anyone. But in practice, that just wouldn't have worked. Apart from anything else, I would have gone nuts staying in that long with an active, inquisitive seven-year-old, who wanted to see where he was living and understand where everything was.

In short, I ignored their advice. Being able to go and play in the park allowed us to develop our bond in a positive way and start as I meant to go on.

At this point, we were very definitely in the honeymoon period that you hear adopters describe. The plan or hope is that the honeymoon period lasts for a reasonable amount of time. A few weeks would have been fabulous. Ignoring the advice to do nothing for two weeks may have had *something* to do with our honeymoon period ending so quickly (coming up soon, on the morning of

Day 14). I'll never know if that was the case and to this day believe I did the right thing.

Day 14

So the third day of living together was an *interesting* day. Munchkin had woken up twice in the night and I'd found him watching TV at 1am and 4.15am. Both times, I'd taken him back to bed and explained he can't watch TV in the middle of the night. Both times, he ignored me. He wouldn't accept that he couldn't. The second time, I'm not sure he went back to sleep, and he appeared in my room wide awake at 5.30am. Without nearly enough sleep and my brain not fully functioning, I was pretty tired that day to say the least. The lack of sleep and emotional exhaustion started kicking in.

Though the morning seemed to be going okay, I sensed something was wrong. I'd told him that we were going to get his new school uniform that day and it appeared to be worrying him, but I was finding it hard to tell, given I didn't know him well enough yet. He was and is excellent at hiding his feelings. Inside, I knew it was too early to be going out. However, I felt like I didn't have much choice. I wanted to make sure Munchkin had his uniform for when he started school a couple of weeks later and couldn't leave it too late, in case the shop needed to order anything in.

The anxiety built up during the morning. Then just as we were about to go out after lunch, and as my cleaner was arriving, the honeymoon period well and truly ended…

Munchkin went into *complete meltdown*, the first of many. It took me by surprise. I hadn't been expecting it and I hadn't seen him behave like it. The only glimpse I'd had was walking back from the park near his foster home. This was *much* worse. His behaviour went downhill fast. He shouted, started being rude, became defiant and finally started throwing things. The training I'd had during the adoption approval process went completely and utterly out the window. I'm not sure it had ever come in to be honest. Since it had been nearly two years since I'd done it, I'd basically forgotten everything I'd learnt, along with everything I'd read. I tried everything I could think of. Talking to him, holding him, putting him in timeout, ignoring him, distracting him, using humour. You name it, I tried it. It took three hours for him to calm down. I have no idea how, but I managed to remain steady throughout all of it. I remember my cleaner saying 'keep going; you're doing brilliantly'. That meant so much, as I felt like a complete failure at that point. I hadn't seen it coming, at least not on that scale. I hadn't been able to help him, to soothe him, to take away his pain – all the things a mother wants to be able to do for her children.

I've had that feeling of failure so many times since then. I'm sure I will keep having it in the years to come.

Finally, once he'd calmed down, we went to the shop to get Munchkin's uniform. He was nervous and clung to me like his life depended on it. That's probably how it felt to him – life or death. The staff in the shop were brilliant and looked after us beautifully. It was wonderful to see him smile as they told him how handsome he looked. And he really did look ridiculously cute. I had that feeling I'm sure all parents get the first time their child puts on a school uniform: a mixture of pride and hope that school will be okay.

When we arrived home from the shop, Munchkin was much more settled and wanted to put all of his uniform on again. We tried it on in different combinations (I'd done the usual new school thing and bought everything!) and he wanted lots of photos. Here's where I learnt how relaxed he is in front of the camera. He posed happily, choosing a variety of positions himself. Remembering the fun we had that day brings a smile to my face. To be able to end an event so well, when it had started out so stressfully, was wonderful.

Days 15 to 17

I woke up the next morning with a major migraine. I'd felt it coming on the night before, but had hoped a good night's sleep would kill it off. Unfortunately not. I felt horrendous and could hardly open my eyes when Munchkin came in at 6am. I said that I didn't feel well and asked him to go play in his room for a bit, which – bless him – he did. For five minutes! He came back in having played – not *quite* what I'd meant – so I told him I had a headache and needed a bit of rest. I sent Munchkin down to watch TV and said I'd be there as soon as I could. Off he went downstairs. Shortly after, I heard a clattering in the kitchen. It bothered me, but I felt that ill I couldn't do anything. A few minutes later, he reappeared in my room with a tray. He'd made me breakfast to help me feel better! Another heart-melting moment right when I needed one. He gave me the food, went to get something for himself, then curled up in bed beside me. I managed to eat some bread and hide the fact that I felt truly sick. For me, eating is usually kill or cure. I crossed my fingers and prayed it be the cure today. Munchkin sat quietly beside, clearly concerned, while I tried to reassure him. His ability to care and look after others shone through, which was both lovely and worrying. It was all-too-clear he'd done this many times before.

An hour or so later, I got up and we decided to have a quiet day. In fact, the next few days were fairly uneventful. (Except for the meltdowns he had almost daily, though they became part of life as we knew it.) We did a trip to the supermarket, which went well but confirmed how hard it is to shop with a child! I'd never understood the persistence until that day. I lost track of the number of times I said, 'No, put it back' or 'How come that's in the trolley?' or 'Please stop racing the trolley down the aisle', and began feeling like a parrot. To this day, I prefer shopping by myself because it's a) cheaper and b) quicker. Far quicker! Oh and there's no surprises when you unload the trolley at the till!

The following day was Saturday and we called Munchkin's foster care family to tell them how he was doing. Leaving them had been hard for him. They had a son not much older whom he missed and had tried to talk to via the Xbox a lot that first week. I'd intervene to stop them contacting one another, after advice from his social worker. It was hard explaining to him why he couldn't speak to people he missed and it felt cruel at times cutting him off from everything he knew. When he spoke to them, he told them about his week and the new school uniform. He seemed happy, although there was some sadness at missing them as well. Upset from the call, Munchkin kept talking about his foster family and all the things they had done together, while we spent the afternoon curled up on the sofa together watching movies. He had several years' worth of memories from his time in their care. It was hard seeing him upset and missing them. I know they were a big part of his life, but there was and is a part of me that wants to forget about that and not think about his life before he came here. I know that's not possible but it is difficult talking about them. I suppose in some ways I'm jealous of the experiences they had with him that I will never have.

Part 3
Meltdowns, Milestones and Many a New Experience

Day 18

Munchkin met my brother T for the first time on the Sunday. At that time, T lived locally to us and he came to spend the afternoon at our house. T is a big kid at heart and seeing them interact was just lovely. Munchkin was a little shy to start off with, but it didn't take long until he was chatting away and showing T all of his toys. They both play Minecraft and Munchkin was happy to have someone to play with him who understood what was going on and knew how to play. Video games aren't my strong point!

It was Easter so my brother had come over with an Easter egg, which went down well. That was the first time he'd met anyone other than me in his new life. He appeared to be pleased at starting to meet family and learning more about my life. I hoped that boded well for the future.

Day 19

Today was social worker visiting day. This was to be Emily's first visit since Munchkin had moved in. He demonstrated that he was anxious about it, being defiant, angry and aggressive that morning, which I now believe to be related to not knowing how to express his emotions in any other way. Over the years, I've worked with him to reduce those behaviours and learn how to express his emotions differently. It's still not perfect but we're getting there.

My plan for tidying the house before Emily arrived pretty much went out the window, as I tried to support Munchkin and reduce the fallout. I used distractions and games, which sort of worked.

When she arrived, Munchkin changed suddenly. So suddenly, that I was taken aback. It was like he went into a particular mode especially for her. He knew the ropes, knew what the social worker would want to do and see. He'd done it for so long. Emily stayed for about an hour and talked to us both. Munchkin showed her his room and toys, then told her what we'd been up to. He seemed fine during the visit, only afterwards was a bit quiet. I often wondered what the silence meant during those times and how he was feeling. Frequently, he would go completely sullen and it took me a long time to understand that was his way of coping and sorting out his feelings.

Day 20

That afternoon, a friend of mine popped round to say hello. Again, this was no-no in the world of social workers and I'd been told it was best to not introduce him to anyone too soon. Munchkin was curled up on a chair watching TV and appeared to hardly notice my friend, although I have no doubt he listened to every word and knew exactly what was going on. His only real acknowledgement of her was when she gave him an Easter egg. Funnily enough, he managed a few words at that point. He was so polite and appreciative, it made me smile. My friend seemed surprised as well. It's one of those moments that sticks in my mind. After the difficulties of the week, it was a reminder of why I'd adopted and why I was adopting Munchkin in particular. I know not everyone feels love for their child the day they meet them, but I really did. Ever since that day, it's moments like this that I've cherished. They keep you going through the bad times.

My friend didn't stay long, but as soon as she left, Munchkin started asking questions about her. He wanted to know everything: where she worked, what she did, how old she was, how long I'd known her, where she lived, everything. To my surprise, the questions kept coming. Looking back, it makes perfect sense that he wanted to know as much as he could about me and where he was now living.

Day 21

When Munchkin moved in, my parents were in the process of coming back from living abroad. It was over a month before they got to meet their new grandson in person.

My parents had had mixed feelings about me adopting, but have been amazingly supportive ever since Munchkin has moved in. They were understandably concerned, particularly given the stories they'd heard in the press and from other adopters. They were worried about my safety, my career, how I'd manage financially and whether I could cope being a single parent of a child who would undoubtedly need lots of support. I understood those fears completely. In many ways, I had the same worries. Somehow though, I just knew it would be okay. Admittedly, I was a bit naïve about some aspects, when I think back now, but I have managed and we are doing okay.

At the time Munchkin moved in, I was planning on returning to work full time. I can't tell you how ridiculous a notion that was! It may have been possible if he was much younger. I know many single adopters who do work full time. But given his age, it just couldn't have worked. I changed my mind swiftly once he was living with me. I always expected to *want* to go back to work full time and return to my career. I thought I'd be one of *those* women who had it all and I couldn't see myself as a stay-at-home mum at all. Once I was a mum, though, I realised I didn't want to return to a busy, stressful role. But that doesn't mean it didn't take time to accept!

While my parents were still abroad, we talked to them online and Munchkin got to know them a little. The first time we rung them was difficult for everyone. They were nervous (although I doubt they'd admit it), I was nervous and Munchkin was a whole bunch of different emotions! We kept the call short, with Munchkin asking to see their flat, and my dad showing him the view from the window. My parents lived on the seventh floor, and the view over the marina of clear blue skies, tall buildings, water, boats and people was awe-inspiring to Munchkin.

My parents would be sailing back home to the UK, so we were able to follow their trip on the website and keep track of where they were. They rang us from the different ports, and Munchkin loved finding out where they were so he could look it up on the map. I often found him on the iPad seeing where they were that day. His inquisitive nature showed through as he asked about the country they were nearest. Many of the countries they stopped at are now on his list of places he wants to travel. Needless to say, he has a fairly exotic list!

Days 22 to 24

For the next few days, we stayed at home mainly, playing in the garden and continuing to get to know each other more. We went shopping, visited the park. That was about it. I could see Munchkin starting to get worried about school, as he was asking questions, some of which I couldn't answer, which only caused more anxiety. I had wanted him to start at the beginning of term with everyone else, but due to some administrative issues, that hadn't been possible. He'd had an extra week at home, which I think he found as hard as I did!

It was about this time that Munchkin's behaviour started to deteriorate and the meltdowns started becoming more frequent and harder to manage.

At times like this, I tried to remember the training I'd received during the approval process. On one of the days of the four-day training course, a child psychologist taught us about parenting children with trauma. That day will stay me forever. It changed my views on parenting completely and was incredibly powerful.

At the time, I'd been watching a well-known TV programme about a nanny who had a different approach. Through that programme, I thought I had this parenting malarkey sorted, to be honest. Oh, how wrong could I be? These meltdown days served as proof of that. Children who have experienced trauma need a different style of parenting altogether. Timeout, rewards and sanctions, along with other common parenting styles, often don't work and can cause further upset for the child. Although that training day had taught me another parenting style, plus techniques to use, actually putting them into practice isn't as easy as the theory. I learnt the hard way, though, that the techniques taught are definitely the better way to go! As the training day had progressed, I realised that what I was being taught seemed like natural parenting – a common sense approach even – whatever the child's background and family circumstances. Why would you use punitive sanctions against any child?

Despite my best efforts at trying to stay calm, I completely failed at times. Some days it just got too much. I felt awful if I shouted, but it just happened at times. Learning about how to parent is one thing; implementing it is a whole different ball game altogether.

Day 25

I thought it would be good to take Munchkin to visit my parents' home in the UK. It would be one less scary hurdle to jump when we finally met them in person. Plus, he wanted to see where they would be living. We used it as an excuse to go play on the beach, because their English home was by the sea. At this point, I was still *supposed* to be staying at home with him and not going anywhere, but that really wasn't happening! I decided to go for it and, keeping my fingers crossed, off we set.

My brother came with us for the day and we took a kite. Munchkin was familiar with a lot of the journey down, as we'd gone past on our many trips to and from his foster carers during Introductions. It wasn't new to him and he liked being able to point out various milestones. He made my brother sit in the back with him to keep him company. When we got there, he was nervous but his curiosity got the better of him and he wanted to look around. We spent some time looking around my parents' flat at all the family photos, explaining who everyone was. Then we went outside to play. Thankfully, it was a lovely day and Munchkin seemed to relax. Seeing him playing with my brother as they flew the kite, it was if he had known him for years. It occurred to me that from the outside, we probably looked like a normal family: mum, dad and son. Little would anyone know I'd only known my son for three-and-a-half weeks and that was his uncle, not his dad.

Munchkin fell in love instantly with the restaurant where we went for lunch. To this day, he enjoys going there. It took a while for him to decide what to order. (Decisions are not always his strong point as so many parents will understand.) Finally, he went for the burger. When it arrived, his little eyes popped out on stalks. Although it was the child's burger, it was still enormous and Munchkin was small for his age. Somehow, he managed to eat it all, along with the chips, a milkshake and some ice cream. I don't know where he puts all the food he eats. If only I was the same!

There's an amazing playground near my parents' home, which we went to after lunch. Apparently, even on a full stomach, Munchkin can swing round in fast circles and not feel sick. I felt sick just watching him. I took so many photos on that (meltdown-free!) day and love looking at his smiling face in them, especially because that smile disappeared for a few weeks after that day, except on a few rare occasions.

Days 26 to 32

It was Day 26 and I got his breakfast wrong. Apparently, I didn't butter the toast correctly and this upset him. It was how our entire week continued. We were on a fast downhill trajectory and I had no idea what to do to stop it. I remember describing it to my social worker Mary months later as 'a living hell'. It didn't matter what I did, Munchkin said it wasn't right. Of course, it always caused a meltdown of some description.

It was this week that the violence started. The meltdowns became more than just shouting and screaming. It was only a little bit to begin with, the odd item being thrown, the odd kick or hit. I tried not to worry too much, putting it down to anxiety and hoping it would just go away. I told him off and made it clear I wouldn't accept that type of behaviour, but it made no difference at all.

On Day 27, Emily came for a visit, which didn't help one bit. I believe Munchkin thought he would be taken away, associating the social worker with that. We were also visiting the school to plan his start for the following week. Munchkin did not want to go and made that abundantly clear. Emily seemed a little surprised by his behaviour having not seen that side of him before. Thankfully I managed to stay calm. (I'm not sure shouting at him in front of his social worker would of gone down well!) Finally, I managed to get him in the car, while Emily went ahead and told the school I was having problems.

Having gotten him in the car and driven to the school, Munchkin's next stand was refusing to get out. At this point, it became a game of me going around the car to the side he was sitting and him shooting across to the side I came from. It's a game we played a lot before I learnt to just stand there until, eventually, he moved and got out of the car. Yes, it means enduring the stares of all the other mums whose little darlings have happily gotten out of their car that morning. I've learnt to smile and say hello, trying to act as if standing by the open car door is a completely normal thing to do in the morning.

Having urged him out of the car, I virtually (not literally of course) dragged him into school and we joined the meeting. At this point, his angelic side reappeared. I was convinced they all thought I was nuts. I just sat there with a grin plastered on my face thinking, 'Oh yippee, that was fun'.

The rest of the week got worse and worse. I almost couldn't wait until he'd start school and I'd get a break, even if getting him there would likely be hell. Later, I described it to Mary as the most horrendous week I'd had in my life. Every day was full of meltdowns, increasing levels of aggression, screaming, crying and defiance.

My other problem during this time, and ever since he'd moved in, was finding him watching TV at all hours of the night. Regularly, I would wake up anywhere between 1am and 5am to hear the TV on downstairs. I'd go down and find him curled up watching it, determined to stay there. Eventually, he would go back to bed and fall straight to sleep, while typically I lay awake for the rest of the night. To solve the problem, I told Munchkin he couldn't go downstairs before 5.30am. That's still early, I know, but he was always up then, so it was a compromise. It didn't work. I moved it to 5.45am. That didn't work either. I was still finding him downstairs before the time I'd allowed. This carried on over the next few months until I decided that he had to come in and see me every morning at 6.30am before he could go downstairs. He didn't like it but it seemed to work. We still do it this way. He comes in at 6.30am *ish* (if 6am counts as 6.30), wakes me up, says hi and asks to go downstairs. It's a good way for us to reconnect in the morning, even if it's a little early for me at the weekends.

Day 33

By the time Munchkin had been at home with me for three weeks, we were both more than ready for him to be in school. Being together 24/7 was not ideal.

During our visit to school the previous week, we'd agreed that he would go half days for the first week and see how he went. His first day he was up and dressed early, which amazed me. I hoped it was a good sign. We went to the school and everything seemed fine until we got there. That's when his nerves and fears took over. It was heart-breaking seeing him so upset as I struggled to get him out of the car. Finally, I managed to get him through the school gate and into reception, where – thankfully – they were there waiting for him. After much crying and clinging on, I released his vice-like grip and handed him over. Fighting back my own tears, I said lots of 'you'll be okay' and 'I'll see you at lunchtime' and left. My head knew I was doing the right thing, but my heart was struggling with putting him in such a distressing position. The relief I thought I'd feel at having some me-time had vanished.

When I picked him up at lunchtime, he'd clearly had fun, but was also ready to come home. He'd been given two buddies for the day, who he said were nice. He also came home with an invitation to a joint birthday party, which I thought was lovely and so thoughtful of the boys. Munchkin seemed pleased.

The next few days seemed okay. On the Wednesday, he even stayed for the whole day to join in a big sports event. I went along to watch and he looked like he was enjoying himself, but his lack of sporting prowess was apparent! Before then, I'd not had anything to compare his abilities to, but that day it was obvious he wasn't a natural sportsman, at least not at that point. He is much better now, but I'm not sure sport will ever be his specialism, even though he enjoys playing. After that day, Munchkin was desperate to do full days. Having discussed it with his teacher, we agreed he would start, as he seemed keen. I thought he was coping well. Oh, how wrong I was!

Day 36

Getting him to school in the following few weeks became harder and harder. Some mornings were absolutely fine; others a complete stressful disaster. I never did know what caused the disastrous days. Though I'm sure there was a reason, I never worked it out, instead learning to just deal with those mornings as best I could.

Adopting Solo

Day 36 was one such disastrous day. I rang the school that particular morning to let them know I was having trouble. I'm lucky I found such a supportive and helpful school that understood Munchkin's needs. I'm appreciative of their support and it makes so much difference having them on my side rather than having to fight them. I said I'd be there when I got there and his teacher even offered to fetch him himself, if I thought that would help. I declined, as I didn't want Munchkin thinking that would happen every time he kicked off. However, the teacher stayed on the phone for a bit to guide me. Eventually I managed to get Munchkin out of the house. In hindsight, it must have only taken 30 minutes, so quite quick, relatively speaking! His next stand was to refuse to put on his seatbelt. When he finally did, I started to drive and he undid it again, so I immediately stopped the car. (Luckily, it was safe for me to pull over.) I waited for what seemed like an age for him to redo it and then drove off. His next plan of attack was to start kicking the back of my seat and hitting me. I ignored him and kept driving. We got to school and I pulled up right outside. Shaking at this point, I was thankful that the headteacher came out and got him out of the car. Munchkin wasn't impressed but did get out and go into school with her. I stood there, took a few deep breaths, then followed him in. We all had a chat in her office and then Munchkin went to class.

When I got home, I collapsed on the sofa with a Diet Coke and watched daytime TV. I decided it was too early for anything stronger! When it was that bad in the morning, it was exhausting. I felt like I had to be one step ahead the whole time to try and manage the situation, but I didn't know which direction he would go next, making it feel nigh on impossible. I ended up just having to react and hope I was doing the right thing. I put myself under pressure to get him there on time and I'm sure that made everything worse as Munchkin would have picked up on my stress.

The school became used to me ringing in the mornings and telling them I'd be there when I could. Some days it would take an hour to get Munchkin out of the house once we were ready. Some days only a few minutes. Other days he would refuse to get dressed, although I had several hours to work on that, given he was up by 6.30am each day!

This pattern became more and more stressful. Apart from the support of the school, I tried ringing Social Services for help several times, but got little response. I also had Mary and her social work team to depend on, who were great. Without them, it would have been a lot harder and they were able to push for further help. Between my phone calls and theirs, we were able to get things moving for more support.

Day 39

Going to school wasn't where it ended. Shower times were beginning to get stressful too. I was insistent that Munchkin had a shower or bath every day, working on the logic that I could reduce it to less than daily once he got used to the routine. Then as a teenager, there was a chance he'd only get a shower or bath once a week, but I'd tackle that later.

The shower meltdowns looked like 45 minutes of shouting, violence and defiance, which was awful. I hated seeing him that way, some unknown deep-seated trauma causing him real pain. It was times like that I didn't know if we'd get through, as I didn't know what to do to help him. I would dread it too and didn't always respond well, which only served to make it worse. Unknowingly, Munchkin managed to push my buttons. Keeping a lid on those frustrations wasn't easy and I couldn't manage it every time. Thankfully the situation is usually much better these days, because I learnt to change how I approached shower time and avoid the sense of dread. I'm much calmer and step away if I see things starting to bubble. I went back to nurturing him, rather than fearing shower time, helping him in the shower and afterwards, which led to improvements.

Once he'd gotten in the shower, he was fine. Then began the process of trying to get him out. This particular occasion was no worse than any other really; it just came on top of another particularly testing day. By the end of it, I was tired, tense and desperate to get Munchkin into bed so I could have some time to breathe and unwind. My responses during this shower meltdown were less than brilliant, which only escalated his behaviour.

Ultimately, we managed to resolve it and the day ended with story time and a hug. *At least he went to bed calm*, I thought, as I went downstairs feeling bad for the way I'd managed everything and vowing to improve.

Day 43

This is the day Munchkin decided he wasn't going to school. He got himself up, made breakfast and went straight on the iPad, his favourite 'toy' to use. I found him eating his cereal on the sofa and reminded him that breakfast should be eaten at the table. (From the start, I was clear we'd sit up to the table for all meals.) Pointing out that he knew this probably didn't help his mood.

A little later, Munchkin joined me in the kitchen to make his packed lunch when I asked him to, much to my surprise. That was about 7.45am and I thought he was going to be okay that morning. Once we'd finished, I reminded him of the time and asked him to get dressed, at which point everything changed. Munchkin refused, saying that he wasn't going to school; he was going to spend the day at home on the iPad. I replied that he was going to school and would only stay home if he was poorly, in which case he would spend the day in bed, not on the iPad.

He spent the next 30 minutes refusing to get dressed and getting increasingly angry. I tried to encourage him, but as his anger worsened and he became aggressive, I shut myself in my bedroom. I hoped he would calm himself down once I was removed from the situation and he could self-soothe. That usually worked. On this occasion, it didn't seem to make any improvement to his temperament, but when I came out, he was at least partially dressed. I threatened to remove the TV that his foster carers had given him as a leaving present from his room. Not one of my greatest moments, in hindsight. As I took the TV downstairs, he kicked off. I spoke to him quietly and tried to tell him to calm down. (Again, I know now that's a useless technique.) At this point, Munchkin admitted he didn't know why he was angry and couldn't calm down. I shut myself in the lounge to stop him hitting and kicking me, but he was banging into the door so hard I was more worried he would hurt himself, so opened it.

Finally, when he started to calm down, I rang the school to let them know we would be late. As I went to put Munchkin's scooter in the car, he locked me out. It hadn't occurred to me that he would do that! He put the chain on so there was no way I could get back into the house. Instead, I got into the car and pretended to drive off, at which point he came running out. I managed to catch him before he could go anywhere and put him into the car carrying him like a baby and giving him a bagel to eat. The journey to school was uneventful after that.

Again, the Headteacher came to get him out of the car and eventually, between the two of us, we coaxed Munchkin into school. That day, after school drop-off, I decided I'd earned a trip to a local café, ordering myself a large hot chocolate and even larger piece of cake! It was my way of coping with what had happened and centring myself.

I was dreading picking him up from school that day, but contrary to my expectations, he was absolutely fine. We played games together that afternoon. And though shower time was tricky as usual (I may be slightly understating it), he got in eventually.

In bed, Munchkin asked lots of questions about the adoption process, like whether I was adopting him yet, and whether it was official. He'd obviously been worrying about it, which explained his behaviour that morning. Then he quizzed me about my parents, who he was due to meet for the first time the next day. I hadn't realised the extent of his worry, because he'd spoken to them a lot on Facetime; I'd concluded that he would take it in his stride when he said he was looking forward to it. But it must have been getting too much.

Day 44

Despite the lead-up to the day, meeting my parents for the first time actually went well. I tried hard to play down the day, as I didn't want any meltdowns if we could avoid it.

We were going my parents' house, because Munchkin had been there before and enjoyed being at the beach. He seemed happy to be going and we had no meltdowns in the morning, which surprised me, to be quite honest. When we arrived, Munchkin was understandably cautious going in, but I was proud of how he handled it. He managed to keep the nerves under control. Although he hid behind me when we first got there, once he realised it was okay and had said hello, he came out and started chatting away. He was the centre of attention and he does like that. He also loves questions! Around the house he went, looking at the photos, asking about the people in them, wanting to know who everyone was. And not just their names, but a full-on history of them. Maybe he was checking I'd given him correct information!

We decided to go out for lunch to the restaurant we'd gone to when I brought him down the first time with my brother. Munchkin enjoyed it as much the second time and behaved well. After lunch, we had great fun at the play area. (Personally, I *love* the zipwire.) Munchkin took photos with my mum's camera, which he got a bit attached to and didn't want to stop taking pictures. It caused a bit of an issue, until I managed to distract him with binoculars. He got bored with those after a while. Problem avoided! Leaving was surprisingly easy too, considering he didn't usually cope well with transitions.

Back at home, it became clear he'd been holding himself together, because it all came tumbling out at bedtime. I was proud of him in many ways for keeping a check on his behaviour while we were out, but I'd felt a sense of dread and worry that this might happen. When it started, I held him tightly in my arms, rocking gently as he screamed. He tried to fight out of my embrace, but not hard, which I took to mean he didn't really want to get away. He started to calm down after a few minutes, but decided that he didn't want to live with me because I didn't let him have enough chocolate brioches. Then it was because we didn't read for long enough at bedtime. Then it was because he didn't want a family. *Then* he said he'd had a lovely day and asked to see my parents again! He followed up with 'could it be before they die?' and I burst out laughing, replying that I hoped they'd be around for a long time yet.

Eventually, Munchkin settled and went to sleep, leaving me thinking about all the worries that must be going through his head, maybe fears that this was too good to be true, or that it would all come to an end. I can find these conversations hard to deal with when he says he doesn't want to be here anymore. I don't know how many times I can keep saying, 'It's forever. You're safe.' That never became any easier over the years. Usually, I manage to bite my tongue (literally at times!) and respond in a caring way that shows I understand how he is feeling and that it must be hard for him, but others I don't and do end up showing my frustration in not always the best of ways.

Day 55

Munchkin's behaviour had deteriorated gravely by this point. At times, he was still the most adorable child you can imagine. Others, well, a completely different side to him came out. Now that I understand brain development and attachment, it all makes sense, but at the time my knowledge was low. All I knew was I was dealing with a highly aggressive young child and that scared me. His strength when angry was unbelievable and I knew I wouldn't be able to stop him when he got older.

His outbursts had grown in intensity and often resulted in me being hit, kicked, punched and having items thrown at me. If I was lucky, not all at the same time, and just soft items being thrown. On many occasions, I was left covered in bruises.

This particular time, he went on for several hours. I tried everything I could to calm him down, but nothing worked. In the end, I stood there and took everything he could throw at me. I didn't react or flinch despite the pain, as he tried harder and harder to get a reaction. He wanted to prove that I would send him away. Several times he said he wanted to leave, that he hated me, that he wanted to go back to his foster carers. He said he knew I didn't love or want him. I tried telling him that wasn't true, but I know now that logic and reason are pointless when he's like that. Eventually, my lack of reaction caused him to stop. He ran to his room. I sat down and burst into tears, the physical and emotional pain just too much. I don't know how long it was before I gathered myself or how many hours the incident had lasted, but it felt like a lifetime.

Once calm, I went upstairs to find Munchkin under his duvet. He was talking to himself as he so often did in these situations. All negative. At times like these, it's hard to hear what my son says about himself. For a child so young to think like that about himself is heart-breaking. Over time, his negative talk has decreased. I sat on the bed and didn't say anything for a while.

When we spoke, our conversation then went like this:

> **Munchkin:** Go away. I don't want you near me.
>
> **Me:** No, I won't. It doesn't matter what you do. You're not going anywhere. You're my son.
>
> **Munchkin:** I hate you. Go away. I don't want to live here anymore.
>
> **Me:** I understand that, but you're not going anywhere. This is your home now and it will be forever.
>
> **Munchkin:** I'm going back to my foster home.
>
> **Me:** No, you're staying here.
>
> **Munchkin [with his hands over his ears]:** La-la-la-la-la, I'm not listening.
>
> **Me [knowing he was]:** Okay, that's fine, but you are staying here whatever you do. When you're ready, I'll be in the kitchen.

I'm sure I could have handled the meltdown better, but when you're in the middle of it, you don't always remember everything you've learnt. Back then, I didn't know what I know now. I learnt it and I learnt him over time.

After a while, Munchkin came downstairs and asked for a hug. We curled up on the sofa and had a chat. We talked about how he was feeling, although he struggled to put it into words. Then we went over how violence is not acceptable. Afterwards, we carried on with our day; as far as I was concerned, the issue was dealt with. I tried to spend time with him for the rest of the day, although inside it was the last thing I wanted to do, because I was still hurting. Pushing him away was my natural reaction, but that would have served only to make me feel guilty, as I knew it wasn't his fault that he couldn't express his emotions any better. He didn't want to behave like that. So I spent time with him to show him I understood that.

Part 4
Seeking Our Supporters

Day 57

We had another awful morning and I was at breaking point. By this point, Munchkin's aggression had become a regular occurrence and I just didn't know what to do. The whole morning had been hell.

I'd managed to get him to school at last, after struggling to get him dressed and out the door. I'd somehow made his lunch and dressed myself in amongst all of it, although I'm sure I looked like something the cat dragged in. At school, they asked how I was and I heard myself say 'I'm fine', which couldn't have been further from the truth. (This was most obvious to anyone looking at me!)

I was fighting back the tears. Had I admitted how I felt right then, I don't think I would have been able to hold them back any longer. Once I'd handed over Munchkin, I virtually ran out of the school. By the time I closed the car door, the tears were rolling down my face and I was crying uncontrollably. I sat there and realised we needed help if we were going to get through this. At least, I knew *I* needed help.

From the car, I rang Munchkin's social worker. Thankfully, Emily picked up and heard the full extent of my distress in the moment, which I reckon came as a surprise to her. I'd tried telling her it was bad before now, but my independence and determination to cope had concealed how I was feeling. Hearing me now would've been quite a shock.

Emily listened as I told her about that morning, the meltdowns and everything else that was happening. Immediately, she agreed to help, asking me what I wanted. I remember thinking at the time that it was a stupid question, because I simply didn't know. All I knew was we needed help, not what was best. The social worker suggested therapy. I agreed willingly. Whatever would help us, I wanted it.

It took two weeks to get the therapy agreed and sorted out. I don't know why it took so long. Surely, it's easy to agree such a service? I know there's *process* to be followed, *costs* to be considered, and so on and so forth. On reflection, I was lucky it was agreed so quickly at all, but it's a service where, if you need it, you need it now.

In the meantime, I received a call from Jo at the behaviour service, which was helpful. If nothing else, Jo listened, told me I was doing okay and suggested some strategies. Those strategies turned out to be beneficial, even if just for a short time.

Day 59

After calling Social Services in tears, the next few days weren't so bad. There were plenty of good times, although those are easy to forget among the bad. Nevertheless, Munchkin and I had fun and laughed together. Things seemed normal, whatever 'normal' was.

Adopting Solo

This Saturday was a real low though. Munchkin asked to go on the Xbox and I agreed to an hour. Any longer and his behaviour afterwards was a nightmare. When I went to get him off, he asked nicely for another 30 minutes and I agreed, mentioning that he wouldn't be able to use the iPad or Xbox any more that day. I'm not sure why I agreed, given that I knew what the consequences would be, but that's what happened.

After the extra 30 minutes, Munchkin came off the Xbox without any arguments and we had lunch together. All was good until we started to get ready to go into town. I let him take his bike, but even with that concession, Munchkin was struggling with leaving the house. At length, we got going and he was laughing away absolutely fine. Given that we were going shopping to get some art and craft bits for him, I thought he would stay that way. Oh, how wrong I could be.

The problem seemed to be that he wasn't in the right frame of mind to make choices. We couldn't find the right paints so had to get something just adequate. First, that was okay. For about a minute. Until it wasn't okay and Munchkin had a screaming meltdown.

The walk home I would describe as 'interesting'; 'awful' would be another word. Munchkin got onto his bike, while screaming, then refused to cross the road, leaving his bike and running back towards the shops. I knew walking towards him wouldn't help, so just stood there while people stared at me. I smiled back at them and must have made them feel pretty awkward. Which felt great… I so didn't need people staring right then.

Finally, Munchkin came back and got close enough for me to catch him. I carried him and his bike across the road, which must have looked ridiculous. It was certainly painful. Now we were on the right side of the road I just kept walking knowing he would follow, which he did, albeit keeping his distance. I crossed my fingers that all would be fine once we got home, but it was clear we were not at all on the same page. Meltdown Part Two ensued not long after.

We were in Munchkin's room when he started to get angry. I can't remember what set him off, or what I said, but he kicked me. He apologised nearly immediately afterwards, but then as he was sitting on my lap, he put his hands around my throat suddenly. I stopped him and said he must never do that to anyone again. He tried again. Straight away, I pushed him off my lap onto the bed and stood up, assuming he was trying to get a reaction. I told him I was going to my own room to calm down, because I was hurt and upset. He tried to follow but I held the door shut.

A few minutes passed and I heard him move away from the door, so I walked to the window to look out as I find the view relaxing. Shortly after, Munchkin came in again and I asked him to leave unless he was ready to apologise. He said he wouldn't and went to leave the room. As he did so, he started crying. It took me a second to see they were real tears. Realising he was hurting, I went over to give him a hug. I'm not sure what started his tears. He told me he'd banged his head, but I've no idea how.

Through the tears, he apologised and I rubbed his head better, as we talked about why he must never do what he'd done. He said he missed his birth mum and foster parents, and that that was why he'd behaved the way he had. I told him I understood, making it clear that it didn't excuse his behaviour.

The situation calmed down and we curled up on the sofa to watch a film. But I spent the evening feeling numb. He had scared me and I was worried about him trying to strangle me again, particularly as he got older and stronger. I tried to remember the good part of the day, in between the bad bits, and that night I decided to start a gratitude journal. I bought a notebook a few days later. To this day, each bedtime, I write the positives I've experienced. That night, I knew tomorrow was another day, and I hoped it would be a better one.

Day 60

On Day 60, we saw my parents for my dad's birthday. My brother travelled down with us and we all went out for lunch. Bar some minor issues (apparently, the peas were overcooked), it was a great day. As my dad said, 'Relax and be pleased he even eats peas.' Good point. I found it hard to relax though, because it had been so tough at home. I kept jumping on the smallest of issues, worried they would turn into major meltdowns. Thankfully, they didn't, though it can't have been easy for Munchkin with me constantly criticising him or telling him what to do.

All in all, we have some wonderful memories captured in photos from this day and it was one to remember.

Days 61 to 66

After the meltdown two days earlier, life hit a calm patch and we managed to have some fun together during the half-term break.

Therapy also started. *I can't tell you* how pleased I was at this. With everything getting so difficult, I knew we needed help, if we were going to get through it and become a family. And that meant help for both of us.

Getting therapy had been a bit of a bureaucratic battle, but perseverance paid off. I was thankful it had been a short battle – only about 3 weeks from requesting it to it starting – not that it felt short at the time. I've learnt since that it was a relatively quick process compared to others I've had (and continue to have) with Social Services.

We were having Theraplay and Play Therapy, which I hoped would help us see some improvement. That first session was beneficial, although trying to get Munchkin to engage wasn't always easy. At the time, it meant him trying to take control of everything and manipulate situations to do what he wanted. He was surprisingly good at it! Each session, I learnt games to play and activities to do that helped us build a bond. We still do them to this day.

I'm glad I pushed for the therapy early, as it seemed to help, but not before his behaviour got quite drastically worse.

Day 71

Over the first few months living together, Munchkin had problems sleeping. It was intermittent, so I never could guess when it might happen. Inevitably, it happened when I was exhausted and in need of a good night's sleep!

At Day 71, it became more regular again. Munchkin's trouble sleeping was upsetting him as well. I thought it may be related to the therapy, which was probably bringing up worries for him. If he believed I would send him away, he wouldn't want to build a relationship with me because it would hurt when we were separated. Therapy brought all these emotions to the fore and was proving hard for him. Whenever he had a bad night, I would reassure him that I wasn't cross and that I was there for him.

Day 79

The therapist suggested doing a test called a MIM (Marschak Interaction Method) test, which is a way of understanding your child on a deeper level and finding out their attachment style. The child is videoed telling stories and acting them out with little toys, in our case, with people and animals.

There were 13 stories. The therapist would start and Munchkin would finish the story off. Except he's not very good at finishing things and his stories rambled on. Often the therapist had to bring the stories to an end. I sat there quietly in the background watching. Even I could pick up the recurring themes, but it was so hard listening to him tell them. I didn't want him to see any reaction on my face the few times he looked at me. I hoped I had my best poker face on.

Some of Munchkin's issues and worries became apparent during those tests. He was diagnosed with attachment difficulties by a psychologist who studied the videos. That report has been crucial in understanding his needs, and getting us the right help and support.

I'm sure having those tests done early after he moved in with me made a significant difference to our family, because the report confirmed some of the behaviours I'd been seeing. Until then, I'd felt like I wasn't being heard or believed by some parties involved.

Reading the report also made me think about the list I'd completed all those months ago during the approval process. It made me realise how important it was that I'd been honest to my social worker Mary about how I felt all the way through the approval process, including how family and friends felt, as well as the type of child I wanted. I was asked to complete a checklist of what I would and wouldn't consider (although I was asked to consider a child on my 'wouldn't consider' list). Saying no to certain conditions, actual or possible, or situations the birth mother may have been in had been difficult as I'd gone through the adoption process, but the MIM test made me realise that nobody can guarantee anything. What's more, they don't necessarily know the child well enough to give an adopter all the information. And that's assuming the information is even known.

What was clear was nobody had done much therapy work with Munchkin and hadn't understood his attachment issues. Having the MIM tests performed early on gave me the ammunition to get the right support in place and research everything I could, so that I could help my child, and us as a family.

Day 83

Next came a few good days. After the assessments, it was easier to understand what was going on for Munchkin and what his reactions were about. I read books – so many books – and did research online to learn as much as I could. There seemed to be conflicting advice out there, which was totally unhelpful. Plus, our therapist was quite determined we should go about the issues in a certain way.

On this particular day, Day 83, Munchkin had gone to the barbers with my brother. (I wasn't allowed to take him. Apparently girls don't go to barbers.) It was the first time he was having a haircut since moving in with me and he was desperate for it. Rather amusingly, he kept calling it the butchers, something I picked up from him and say occasionally even now. The two of them went off to look for a new bike too. By all accounts, it sounded like Munchkin was well-behaved.

Not long after he got home, Munchkin had a complete and utter meltdown. In the end, I called T and asked him to come back over, because I was at my wits' end. This episode was awful, getting hit, kicked, punched, bitten. Items, again, were thrown.

I honestly didn't know if I could carry on. I wondered if I'd done the right thing by adopting. I questioned whether I could cope by myself. This was the first time I'd felt like this. Until now, it hard been hard at times, but I hadn't questioned if I could continue. I'd always known it would be hard but I'd been confident in myself that I could do it.

I emailed Social Services once he was asleep to tell them what had happened. I asked for more help and an extension to our therapy. I knew we would need it, if we were going to get through. Later that night, I was lying in bed thinking, worrying. Looking back in my journal from that time, I've written:

'Do I still want this? Yes.

Is it difficult? Yes.

Can I do it? Yes.'

Inside of me, I knew I would be okay, that we would get through, but that didn't stop the near-daily worry and uncertainty. What I did realise that night was I was changing. I noticed how going back into a stressful full-time job wasn't something that I wanted anymore. Nor would I be able to do that. However, I was also concerned about changing careers at this stage of my life. *Would I manage it with everything else going on?*

I started thinking about other options and investigating what else I could do. I figured out how feasible alternatives would be. I realised if I wanted it enough, I could make something else work, something other than a job. I needed something flexible enough to allow me to support Munchkin in the way he needed me.

That started the search for something new...

Day 86

Munchkin was back to his *early* early mornings. I would regularly find him playing in his room any time from 5am. It worried me. Although he didn't go downstairs until coming in to me at 6.30am, like we'd agreed, it meant he wasn't getting enough sleep. Obviously, that wasn't going to help him cope. I thought about putting him to bed earlier, as his foster carer had done, but I knew that wasn't a great answer. I talked to him about the importance of sleep and why he needed to try sleeping later or at least stay lying in bed. I believe he *sort of* understood, but he seemed to have an internal alarm clock that would wake him early, whatever time he went to bed. He tried to stay in bed a few mornings after that talk, *I think*, but then went back to getting up and playing. I decided it wasn't something I could fix.

It also wasn't a priority, so I simply hoped it would sort itself out over time. Two years on, he's still usually up between 5.30 and 6am, but now he's pretty good at staying in his room until he's allowed to come see me and go downstairs at 6.30am.

Day 87

For the three days in the lead-up to Day 87, life had been wonderful. It was like I had a different child. Munchkin appeared much happier. After the difficult weekend, we'd had an emergency therapy session, in which the therapist had used puppets to talk about experiences in foster care and to get Munchkin to acknowledge that his behaviour wasn't acceptable. The puppets talked about how they should behave, so they can stay with their forever family. It seemed to work and help him to understand. For a few days anyway.

On this particular morning, Munchkin decided he wasn't going to school. It was the end of the week and he was tired. We were late getting there and we went straight in. The headteacher happened to be outside and caught us on the way into class, so we went into her office for a chat. She asked Munchkin's teacher and the SENCo to join us. It took five minutes just to get Munchkin to sit down on a chair and not hide behind me. Understandably, he didn't want to be there. He was wound up, anxious. I imagine he thought he was about to be told off, because he knew his behaviour hadn't been acceptable that morning. I had the marks to prove it.

Instead, his teacher was brilliant. Talking to Munchkin, he said he wasn't happy and expected more from him. The SENCo suggested a 'stop, think' card to help him when he got angry or distressed. Munchkin liked that idea, so later that day, he made one with the Learning Mentor. It has a picture of me, his teacher and the headteacher on it looking stern and the word 'stop' in capitals on the other side. The idea was that, when Munchkin was starting to melt down, I would hold it up in front of me. We hoped it would lead him to stop and think about what he was doing. (As a side note, this did work a few times, then he just ignored it.)

After our meeting, he went off to class. When I collected him that afternoon, he was lovely. In fact, the whole weekend was lovely. We had another therapy session and lit candles to represent everyone who loved him. This was powerful for Munchkin. Afterwards, we went to my parents' and played on the beach. He was having a great time until he fell over (thankfully right by my parents' front door). He screamed for 15 minutes and you'd have thought his leg had fallen off! It was only a graze, but it was clear to me that he needed lots of nurture. I'll be honest; getting close to a screaming child wasn't much fun. When I finally helped him calm down, he let me clean and dress the graze. Up to that point, I hadn't been allowed to touch it, even though he was screaming at me to stop the bleeding (there wasn't any) and put a plaster on! I do so love those moments when you can't do right for doing wrong…

Transitions were still hard for Munchkin. He hated leaving my parents' house and coming home. He hated leaving or going anywhere actually, but was almost always absolutely fine as soon as we left. That evening, he did everything possible to delay our departure. Once we got on our way, we managed to stop at some shops to buy him a few bits, including a blackout blind which I prayed would mean better sleep. He went to bed that evening absolutely fine.

Day 91

The blackout blind was working! I couldn't believe I hadn't thought of it before. He already had blackout curtains, but the blind made a significant difference, and Munchkin slept until 6.15 that morning. Ridiculous how pleased I was about that. It didn't work every morning thereafter, but it definitely made a difference.

Day 96

I love horse-riding and have ridden for most of my life. I prefer riding horses that are full of beans, so if I don't focus I'll fall off. It's more fun to ride the lively ones and I find it a great way to de-stress.

Sarah Fisher

Every year, I take my brother horse-riding for his birthday. This year, I wanted to take Munchkin as well, so I booked a beginners ride, which goes round the farm. My parents joined us too. When we got there, Munchkin was understandably anxious. Horses aren't exactly small and you do have to be careful. I'd decided I wouldn't ride, but would lead Munchkin round to help him feel safer.

We got him on his horse without too much of a problem, and once he was on, you could visibly see he was okay. The mistake I made was getting him on his horse first, because it meant he had to wait for the others to get ready. While we were waiting, Munchkin started to get anxious. Then wanted to get off. All totally understandable. Particularly when the horse started to get bored and was ready to go as well. Once we set off, though, he grinned from ear to ear for the whole hour. He asked questions about how to sit properly, how to control the horse and told me off for walking too slowly! The second half of the ride, they get to trot up the side of some fields. I hadn't thought about that when I decided to walk. It's quite a long way, a bit of a hill and the ground isn't that even. On top of that, I was in wellies. Thankfully we were at the back but I was told in no uncertain terms to keep going and not stop or slow down. We made it to the top of the hill, me completely out of breath, bright red, and wishing I exercised more... Munchkin grinning like mad.

He had loved it! That meant I got the joy of doing the hill trot several more times. I assured myself I felt better for the exercise at the end. It was a great afternoon of fun with the family and the first of many occasions that we've ridden together. Over time, Munchkin has increased his confidence around the horses and loves helping out afterwards. We found something he enjoys and that we can do together.

Day 101

Another activity I love is growing my own vegetables and I do it nearly every year. Nothing exotic or complicated. Just a few spuds, tomatoes, cucumbers, courgettes, all in tubs or hanging baskets, and usually mainly eaten by slugs. I enjoy it. There is something quite wonderful about eating home-grown vegetables.

It's not something Munchkin had ever done before. Just after he moved in, he helped me plant the potatoes. I could see why he was sceptical and didn't think they would grow. It *does* just look like you're planting potatoes in soil! Over the weeks, though, they grew and eventually flowered. Munchkin was half-interested, which was good enough for me. I recognised that the flowering part isn't the most fascinating bit. When they were ready to be picked, though, he was cautious, right until he realised it involved digging through the dirt to find them. Getting mucky he could do!

Now, I'm quite particular about things like this. As much as anything, I didn't want too much mess or any damaged potatoes after managing to get them to grow. As a result, I was *really* struggling to just relax and let him enjoy it. I took a few deep breaths and tried hard not to keep nagging him to do it the 'right' way. We ended up with several bowls of potatoes and a lovely photograph of the two us basking in our growing success.

Now, I'd assumed because Munchkin liked potatoes, he would happily eat the ones we had just picked. Not so! According to Munchkin, 'Potatoes from the shops are different. They don't grow them like that. You can't eat things out of the soil'. Patiently, I tried to explain that they were exactly the same, if not nicer, because they were fresher. He was having none of it. Potatoes are supposed to come in plastic bags. Clearly, I had my work cut out.

This is where some of my Mummy Tricks came in handy. I bought some potatoes from the supermarket and swapped some with the ones we'd grown. He happily ate them, though not without checking the supermarket bag to make sure some were missing! To this day, I haven't told him what I did. It's a bit like grating carrot into the spaghetti Bolognese. I didn't tell him about that for ages either. It's lucky he loves vegetables, but it never does any harm to get in a few more.

Day 113

On our journeys back and forth during Introductions, we passed the same castle many times and Munchkin decided he wanted to visit. We picked a day and our trip was brilliant. We were on our way home from a therapy session, so having some fun seemed like a good idea. It was lovely sunny day too. Perfect for castle-visiting. Had it been raining, I'd have had to come up with another plan.

The gardens were beautifully designed and we had fun playing in the maze and looking at all the flowers they grew there. It was quite a show. I was surprised at how interested Munchkin was, captivated by the colours and styles of plants, and figuring out how the fruits and vegetables grew. I took an excessive amount of photos that day!

Inside the castle was just as interesting. The family still live there and you're allowed to visit some of the areas they use now. The splendour and decadence of it all is breath-taking. You can even tell how it used to be long ago. On that day, we decided we'd both like a big house, but maybe not a castle! Munchkin was intrigued by the older part of the castle as well, and to my amazement, read some of the information boards. (I'm more a look and walk on girl!) He wanted to take it all in, and was asking questions and making comments. It was wonderful to see him so clearly engaged and enjoying it, from an educational perspective as much as us having a good time together. I was literally dragging him out three and a half hours later because it was closing!

Obviously, a trip to the gift shop on the way out was required. Like many children, adopted or otherwise, he wants to buy the entire shop. I've always been strict about how much he can spend at times like this. I'm fortunate in that money isn't tight for us, but I'm also aware of not spoiling him, especially being mindful of his limited ability to cope with lots of material possessions. As with so many children, his want of new toys etc. isn't because he truly wants them, but a desire to fill an unmet need without knowing how else to fill it, or even being conscious that it exists.

Day 117

Something had been building for a while and I could sense that Munchkin was not right. However, I had no idea what was wrong and he didn't seem to know or be able to express it either. That morning it all came out.

I can't describe what happened in detail: partly because I don't remember the detail; partly because it wouldn't be fair on anyone involved. All I can liken it to was a volcano erupting and I was stuck in the lava flow with no way of getting out. Everything I tried made the situation worse. Occasionally, I thought we'd found a way through, but 10 or 15 minutes later, if it was even that long, it started up again. I was concerned about my safety and Munchkin's, the violence was so bad. I tried every trick in the book, literally everything I could think off. I shut myself in my room, until he was banging so hard I was worried he would hurt himself. I tried holding him, without any progress. I even tried just standing there, taking the hits and kicks. He was clearly so distressed that morning that he couldn't calm down no matter how hard he tried. Eventually, I went outside. He locked the door, put the chain on, and I couldn't get back in with just the key. Since he'd locked me out before and I knew it might happen again, I'd taken a back door key too.

I continued following the advice I'd been given, which was not getting anyone else to come over and intervene. I'd done that before and it had worked well, but I'd since been told that didn't help build the bond between us. The theory goes that he needs to see me as the authority figure. Getting someone else to help would make my son think I couldn't cope and that he was in control. I know now that this advice just isn't right. Having support and people who can intervene at times like this is crucial. It can calm situations down quicker, or at least help to keep everyone safe.

My difficulty that day was that very few people knew about the violence at that point. Again, not good. I've learnt so much since then and really wish I'd known it sooner.

This meltdown lasted for three and a half hours, by which time I was in tears on my driveway, Munchkin distressed but starting to calm down. I didn't think I could carry on being a parent. It was the lowest day I've had in the whole time he has been with me and the only time I thought seriously about throwing in the towel. Although inside I knew I never would.

It took several calls to our therapist, his social worker, and the emergency duty team, as well as a desperate plea for help before anyone arrived. I had to fight for it. When I got back in the house, I told Munchkin it was lunchtime and that afterwards someone was coming to look after him so I could go out. He was visibly upset, worried, anxious and scared. I believe he thought he would be taken away.

The two Social Services people attended a few hours later and I went out for an hour. I ate a lot of cake in that time and figured I'd earned the biggest hot chocolate with extra whipped cream and marshmallows that I could find. The respite gave me time to centre myself and think about how to move forward.

When I got back, the Social Services team had done some work with Munchkin on his anger and created some cards for him to hold up to say how he was feeling – angry, sad, happy. They had also talked to him about the violence and explained it wasn't acceptable. He gave me a hug and said sorry. After the duty team left, I tried to carry on as normal. I'd made the decision to not address the behaviour until the following day when I'd had some proper time to decide what to do. We watched a film that night, like we usually did on a Saturday, and he went to sleep. He must have realised how bad it had become, because he was as good as gold for the rest of the evening.

Looking back, it was during this time I started to realise how important my support network was and would be moving forward. Until then, I hadn't given it much thought. My social worker had talked about it so much – so much! – during the approval phase. To tell the truth, I thought she'd been overegging it a little. A lot in fact. Naturally, I'm highly independent and don't rely on others at all if I can help it. I've always believed in standing on my own two feet and finding a way through. That's not to say that I haven't got help when I needed it; just that I tended to find that help in other ways, not by asking family or friends. Over the last few years, I've slowly accepted that asking for help is possible and not a weakness. Often, people are glad to help when I ask for it, so I'm getting better at asking.

Frankly, you cannot overestimate how much help and support you need, and how hard it can be to get it at times, especially from Social Services and other professionals. Friends and family may find it impossible to understand what you're going through, especially if they've never worked with or parented a traumatised child. During the approval phase, my social worker and I talked about who my friends are, where they live, and whether they'd be on the end of the phone in the middle of the night if I needed them. At the time, I believed they would be. Thankfully, I've been proved right. My friends *have* been incredible. I have spent time explaining to all of them why I parent the way I do and I'm sure that's made a difference.

Day 118

On the morning of Day 118, Munchkin came into my room as usual and got into bed for a cuddle. I guessed he needed some reassurance, which I could totally understand. He went downstairs to watch TV and I decided to talk to him at breakfast, when we were both sitting at the table. I talked about what had happened and it became clear he didn't remember all of it. I imagine the rage inside him was so strong that it blocked his memories. It wasn't an easy conversation as you can imagine. Again, I made it clear that violence was unacceptable and I would not be treated like that again. He asked if he was going to be taken away. I remember pausing, realising that I needed to be careful in my answer. I responded by reiterating that we had to stop the violence, because although I didn't want him to leave and wanted him to stay, I would not tolerate violence. I added that it might not be my decision, if it continued. He seemed to accept that.

We talked some more and decided to try a reward chart for his behaviour for a month. I know, I know. Reward charts don't work. They aren't recommended usually. But back then, I didn't know that and was willing to try anything. Plus, the therapist *had* recommended them, so I thought it was worth a shot. We agreed what his reward would be and it was big. I wanted to make it something he wanted a great deal so he would work for it. I explained that if he could avoid being violent for a month, the length of the reward chart, then that showed he didn't need to use violence to express how he's feeling at all. He said it would be hard, which I acknowledged, adding it was important. And so, the reward chart was drawn up and put on the kitchen wall.

After that conversation, life carried on as normal. We spent the afternoon at the stables, because it's something we can do together and horses are great therapy. The issue was raised at school on Monday morning when we met with his teacher, who was incredibly supportive as always, and then it was put to bed. I don't believe in constantly going over things.

Day 120

Following the meltdown at the weekend, both of our social workers turned up for a meeting about how to move forwards. When I'd called everyone on the Saturday, I'd asked for Munchkin to be taken away, saying that I couldn't do it anymore. And at the time, I'd meant it. I didn't know how to carry on, or if I even *could* carry on, especially given his violence.

During the meeting, both social workers asked how I was and what had happened. I had bruises on my right arm and both legs. When I explained, Mary was brilliant, completely supportive of me. Munchkin's social worker Emily asked if the bruises had been caused by him and I confirmed. Her face was a picture, clearly shocked. Up until then, I'm not sure she'd really believed me when I said he was hitting me.

In the meeting now, I made it crystal clear that I didn't want Munchkin to go, but that I did need *real* support. I agreed with my social worker when she remarked that things might not have gotten so bad if I'd followed my gut instinct and called for help sooner. We agreed I would keep having more therapy, which at the time seemed to be helping. It was a tough discussion, but made me even more determined to make it work. Sending him back to care wasn't the answer for him or for me. We simply had to get through this somehow.

Day 126

On this day, I popped into my employer for a meeting. Initially, I'd planned on being back at work in September and the time had come to start the conversation. It felt strange being back in the building.

It was a lovely warm day, but I had on long sleeves and trousers to hide all the bruises. Sitting chatting to my boss, he told me how well I was looking, despite the stress he knew I must be under. I don't think I'll ever forget that conversation. When I'd started my adoption leave, I was stressed enough. The sort of stressed that makes you look pale and downtrodden in your whole demeanour. Now I felt exhausted, but strangely not stressed, at least not in a way I recognised, although in reality I must have been. Life was so different and I felt a sense of fulfilment and happiness I hadn't felt before. I was happy to get the compliment, even though it was a bit at odds with how I felt.

Day 133

We went to stay with one of my oldest friends S and her children B and D for a few days. It was a long drive up there and during it I got bombarded by questions.

Munchkin: How long have you known S for?

Me: About 20 years, sweetheart.

Munchkin: Really?

Me: Yes, we met at uni.

Munchkin: Wow, that's a really long time. [slight pause] I wasn't even born then. My birth mummy would have been though. She's about 30 now I think.

Me: No, you weren't born then. Yes, I think your birth mum is about 30 now, so she would have been born then.

Munchkin: What's S like?

Me: She's lovely. You'll really like her and her children. You'll meet her husband as well, who's also nice. He'll be at work so you won't see much of him.

Munchkin: And her children are called B and D?

Me: Yes, B is the same age as you and D a year older.

Munchkin: Okay. Do they have pets?

Me: No.

And on it went for several hours. The only time the conversation changed was when he urgently needed the loo. (Why do they always wait until you have just passed the service station to tell you they need the loo?!)

When we arrived, S came out with D and B. I got out of the car and had to coax Munchkin to join us, as he was so nervous about meeting them. It didn't take long. Within 10 minutes, he was happily playing with them in the garden. It was so lovely to see him enjoying himself with children he had only just met, particularly that he was allowing himself to play and not let his anxiety take over.

The following day we went to the coast for the day and it was all going really well, until it came to leaving the beach. First, Munchkin refused to get out of the sea. Then, he wouldn't get changed. He didn't want to leave, as he was enjoying himself. I didn't handle this as well as I could have at all. It was out in public, so I didn't know what to do. I felt out of my depth and actually embarrassed that I couldn't manage my son's behaviour. I made the mistake of saying he couldn't have an ice cream on the way back if he didn't do as he was told. He didn't do as he was told, but I know now that he couldn't, because he was in such a state of psychological arousal that he couldn't make decisions or do as I asked. Telling him he wouldn't get an ice cream didn't help. It only served to shame him when the other children were eating theirs.

He still remembers that day, and what he remembers most was not getting the ice cream. I still remember it too, as a lesson in what not to do. I feel awful even now about shaming him that day, but I know what to do instead these days, and most of the time I manage it.

The rest of our stay passed without incident. We even managed the goodbyes without any major issues, although he didn't want to leave.

Day 137

The summer holidays hadn't been too bad up to this point. The reward chart was going well and Munchkin was proudly adding his stars to the chart every day. I'd gone a few weeks without being hit and it felt like we were making progress.

The major blip came during a therapy session when adoption was described to him as cutting a piece of paper in half and permanently severing all ties with his birth parents. I was so shocked that I didn't know what to say. I couldn't believe it was thought appropriate to say this to a seven-year-old. While I understand that this is what happens *legally*, Munchkin was worried about it, because he wanted to stay in contact with his birth family. And I had promised him we'd do this through the letterbox system. This explanation during therapy was an unhelpful setback. It took me a good 10 days to get him back on an even keel again. It also caused the only blip he had on his reward chart. He still got his reward for doing so well though; I didn't want him to learn that one blip means complete failure.

Day 139

At this point, I realised going back to work in September just wasn't going to happen. Munchkin needed me and I wasn't ready to restart work. I plucked up the courage to tell my employer and they were okay about it. I renegotiated a new earliest start time of November, and said possibly not until January. Having sent the email, a weight lifted off my shoulders. That's how I knew I'd done the right thing.

Part 5
Summer Holiday Success!

Day 141

It was a glorious August day, so I decided to take Munchkin to the local animal rescue centre for the afternoon. The rescue centre is a wonderful place where you can wander around and see the animals, and there's a playground and café too. Knowing Munchkin's love of animals, it seemed like a great idea and I hoped it would help him relax a little. He was worried about going somewhere new, as usual, but we avoided meltdowns that day. When we got there, he loved it. We looked at the birds, including the talking parrot that made me jump, much to Munchkin's amusement. We visited the horses, stroked the donkeys and saw the cats. We walked through the woods and this time it was Munchkin's turn to jump as the ducks and geese appeared from nowhere!

The cats were the flavour of the day though. With two at home, I had no intention of getting any more, but I'm sure you can imagine what happened next. Yes, some rather gorgeous kittens were looking for a new home. Before I knew it, we were signing ourselves up to rehome one of them. I have to say Munchkin's levels of persuasion were second to none that afternoon, although admittedly the kittens *were* cute. As we registered, we were told there would be a six- to ten-week wait so I breathed a sigh of relief in the hope that he would have forgotten all about them by then. Not so much... He talked about them nearly every day.

Day 146

Another trip we took that summer was to Buckingham Palace and Westminster. Getting Munchkin out of the house that morning was awful, as he threw a major meltdown, which I'm convinced was a result of the therapy session the previous week. I thought about joining him and having my own meltdown in the end. By the time, we got to the station, I was dreading the whole day.

To Munchkin's surprise, though, my mum was on the train and was joining us for our trip. His little face when he saw her was wonderful; he was so pleased she was coming with us. When we arrived in London, we walked to the palace, but fear struck Munchkin all over again. Whether it was the number of people, lack of certainty about the unknown or something else, I don't know. And I doubt he knew either. Between mum and me, we managed to calm him down. Taking some photos in front of the palace helped.

We had tickets to go inside and Munchkin was totally enthralled. He loved the special children's audio information guide, which spoke to his inquisitive nature. Luckily, it wasn't too crowded so we had space to look around and Munchkin could go at his own pace. Crowded places can be difficult for him and I was worried his behaviour might deteriorate. While we were inside, Munchkin decided he'd like to live in a big house like Buckingham Palace one day, so suggested I worked hard to buy one. Not sure I'm going to manage to earn *quite* that much though!

After the palace, we walked through St James' Park and around to Westminster. I have a ridiculous amount of photos from that afternoon, because Munchkin got hold of the camera, taking pictures of Big Ben and a traditional red telephone box. I had to pose I don't know how many times and then had to take just as many photos of him. He enjoyed himself, and so did I once I'd relaxed into it and allowed myself to act like a tourist!

Day 151

On another trip to London, we visited London Zoo, where I hadn't been for years. It really is a fabulous place. We spent the whole day seeing all the animals. And I mean *all*. Munchkin was very careful to make sure we had seen *every single one*.

One of the funniest moments was in the monkey enclosure. Walking through, there are big signs that tell you to put everything away, not eat or drink. The signs were clear, but obviously not big enough for everyone. There were lots of small monkeys running around the enclosure, moving like lightning. Several times, we both jumped as one appeared next to us from nowhere. I saw a pair of sunglasses disappear into the bush. Then a young woman standing near us, who I guessed from the way she was dressed might be on a date, reached for a packet in her bag. In a flash, a monkey ran over and straight up her leg to grab the bag. Between the packet she was holding and the short ruffled skirt, the monkey was becoming highly excitable. I don't think

I'll ever forget the look of terror on her face. Even now, it makes both of us laugh when we talk about it, but at the time it made Munchkin decide he'd had enough in the enclosure!

What a crazy amazing day. And notably meltdown-free.

Day 160

Two weeks later, we went for another visit to the animal rescue centre as Munchkin was desperate to go again. While we were there, we went to see where we were on the list for rehoming a kitten. I was dragged in to ask! Munchkin had spent the previous two weeks asking if the centre had contacted me yet. Ah, my plan had failed. He definitely hadn't forgotten!

The lady on reception that day said we would get a phone call when our name came to the top of the list, which might not be for a few weeks yet. Still, we went for a wander round to see all the animals and then sat down for an ice cream in the cafe. At this point, I checked my phone and saw a missed call from earlier that day. I listened to the voicemail which had been left whilst we were driving to the centre. It was the centre saying that we could go and choose a kitten if we were still interested. So in we went and spoke to the receptionist again to say I'd received a call. Then we went to choose a kitten.

Munchkin was so excited that I had to keep reminding him to stay calm around them, so he didn't frighten them. They had a lot of ridiculously cute kittens hidden away out the back. When I saw them, I was smitten. I had to fight my inner desire to take several. Eventually, we chose one and agreed to go back and collect him a few days later.

Adopting a cat was a great way of talking to Munchkin about adoption in general, without talking directly about adopting him. Both of my other cats were adopted too. The eldest was the same age as Munchkin when she came to live with me, so I've often used that as a way of talking about the emotions he must have felt, as well as trying to help him accept everything that happened. Our new kitten had had brothers back in the shelter. I've since heard Munchkin talking to him about how much he must miss them, but that it would be okay because he had a loving home now. It's deeply heart-warming to overhear those conversations.

Day 162

The next couple of days were filled with overexcitement on Munchkin's part. It came at the same time as going back to school, but the excitement of adopting our new kitten seemed to override the fear of going back to school, so it turned out to not be too bad.

We visited school on the inset (or teacher training) day to allow Munchkin the time to see the school again without everyone else there. His Learning Mentor met us and took us to see his new classroom and where Munchkin would be sitting. His teacher had made sure his place was already marked out for him. We showed him his peg and had a look around the whole school so that he felt comfortable again. It seemed to work well to allay any worries.

The following day it was a bit tricky getting him up and dressed, but we made it in on time. Although there were tears, it wasn't too bad by comparison to some mornings. I took him into his classroom and handed him over to the teaching assistant. His Learning Mentor was also there to support. They were brilliant and I rushed off as soon as I'd handed him over, so he wouldn't see me cry. It broke my heart seeing him so upset and I felt like an awful mum, but the school rang mid-morning to say he was fine and chatting away to anyone who would listen about his new kitten!

Day 163

Munchkin was up at 5.30am ready to go and collect the kitten. It took me a while to explain that we were not collecting him until 2pm.

When we got there, he was so excited and couldn't stand still. We had a conversation in the car about being calm around the kitten and following the lady's instructions when we got there. The excitement stayed just that though – excitement – and didn't become anything else.

We went inside and filled out a load of paperwork. Adopting a child seems to be all about paperwork. The whole process involves so much of it. And now *having a child* involves so much more! I can see why parents miss stuff. I often do too; there seems to be a constant flow of forms to sign or read or action, sometimes all three. It seemed that adopting a kitten would be document-intensive too. Paperwork complete, we went to pick up our kitten. The lady opened the door and out came his brother who promptly went and sat in the cat carrier, much to the amusement of us all. He was clearly ready to go to a nice home. Having swapped the cats and collected the right one, we headed off.

Munchkin named the cat Timmy the Tabby. I've since renamed him Killer, which is much more appropriate given his behaviour. More on that later.

We needed to keep him separate from my other two cats for 24 hours. Or at least, that was the plan. Munchkin was so excited and wanted them all to be friends so badly that we managed about two hours before the intros started. It felt a bit like Introductions again, only this time I was the one watching and orchestrating. The cats warily eyed each other up and down. Munchkin kept carrying them towards each other. It was an interesting hour watching him trying to get the kitten accepted. It was a kind of therapy for him in a way. I wondered if he was in some way playing out how he felt when he met me, only he was in a different role. I even heard him saying to Timmy, 'It's okay. I know it's scary going to a new home, but it will be okay'.

The kitten was going to be kept in the living room for the first few days while he got used to us. He wasn't allowed outside for at least two weeks. But it soon became apparent that he had other ideas!

Although Munchkin was excited about getting his own cat, I kept getting told I was mad to have another. And yes, I probably was. Yet it helped Munchkin's progress in settling down and knowing this was his home.

Day 186

It was Munchkin's first birthday since coming to live with me and the first time I'd organised a child's birthday party. I was so worried I'd get it wrong, not do it right, buy bad presents or not make his party fun. I'm sure he picked up on my stress. For him, trying to decide what he wanted wasn't easy either. He hasn't been great at decisions at the best of times, so it took him a while to decide. Eventually, he chose a swimming party, which was great, because it meant I could pay someone else to organise the whole thing!

In the run up, I could see Munchkin fretting about his birthday and the party. It was all new and he didn't know what to expect. I was pleased that everyone he invited could make it and dread to think how he'd have felt if they couldn't. Something I'm relieved I didn't have to deal with.

On the day of his birthday, my parents and brother came over and we went out for dinner. We had the cake I'd made him and all seemed fine. I'd made a fuss of him and decorated the house, so when he went down in the morning, there were balloons and 'happy birthday' signs up. I'm not a big one for birthdays, or Christmas for that matter, and neither are my family, so it was relatively low key, which I'm sure helped him cope. It allowed him to enjoy it without him feeling overwhelmed – key in avoiding meltdowns.

Munchkin, bouncy as children can be on birthdays, loved his presents. And by bedtime, the excitement hadn't worn off. Again, it was interesting (read: blinking hard work) getting him to calm down enough to go to sleep, which he eventually did.

Sarah Fisher

In the middle of the night, I was woken by him calling me. I knew something was up immediately, because usually he comes in to me. Then the smell hit me as I walked into his room. Horrible. I turned on the light to see he'd been sick. Really sick. I was nearly sick myself. Momentarily, my thoughts turned to my mum and I felt sorry for her. Suddenly, I understood why she was so insistent we put towels on the floor if we felt unwell. Tidying up the mess was definitely not something I would want to do again.

The poor little mite looked as awful as I'm sure he felt. He was apologetic and kept saying he didn't mean it. For some reason, he seemed to think he'd be in trouble, which I kept saying he wasn't. I cleared everything up, covered the room in towels, settled him back to sleep and went back to bed myself. In the morning, Munchkin came into me and apologised again, repeating that he was sorry and didn't mean to be sick. Sometimes all you can do is keep reiterating that it's okay and it will finally sink in.

On top of the apologies, Munchkin seemed anxious that I wouldn't let him swim at his party that afternoon. But I did and he was fine. I'm sure it was just too much cake and sweets that caused it, nothing more.

That afternoon, the swimming party went brilliantly; he loved every minute. I managed to avoid getting in the water too – bonus! – and stayed on the side of the pool 'organising'. Although I'm not sure what I organised! My brother was a complete hero in the water with the boys. To be fair, I think he enjoyed acting like a kid as much as they did. And the boys certainly enjoyed jumping on and off him! It was lovely to see Munchkin having such fun with his friends.

On the whole, Munchkin enjoyed the entire experience. But better than anything, he seemed to manage it well. Yes, we had a few moments, but overall he was fine. I'd survived my child's first birthday *and* managed to get it right. Phew!

Part 6
Settling Into A New Normal

Day 201

I was starting to plan a return to work. It was coming up in a few months and I'd agreed with my employer to go back part time. Because of the commute, I was going to do two long days, so I would need to hire a childminder. I managed to find a wonderful lady whose children were at the same school as Munchkin. We agreed that he would start going before I went back to work to get him used to the new routine. It also meant I could do some keeping in touch (KIT) days and get myself organised for returning to the office.

Munchkin was worried – understandable – and didn't want to go, so I took him round to the house for a visit. There, he seemed okay. Munchkin knew the childminder's daughters and other children she looked after from school, which made it a lot easier. On the whole, he likes it there and still goes to her now, including during school holidays. Those holiday days are great fun for him, because the childminder usually takes the children out for the day and he gets to play with the others. Apparently, it's more fun with her than with me! Of course, he has his days when he doesn't want to go and wants to stay by my side, but that's normal and tends to happen when he's feeling insecure about something going on.

Day 211

Bonfire nights are big business where we live. And I *absolutely* relish them. The processions are always brilliant, with everyone dressed up and carrying torches, followed by a huge bonfire, then fireworks. I do love fireworks. There's something about them that keeps me watching, ohh-ing and ahh-ing along. How they make them work I don't understand, but they are impressive.

We watched the bonfire display near us with my parents. The dazzling procession went on and on, with floats and brass bands playing, the local bonfire societies in fancy dress. The bonfire was huge and the fireworks lasted ages. I could see that Munchkin was simultaneously nervous and excited. The number of people was frightening him, then when the fireworks started going off he was outright scared, clinging on to me. I held him tightly and talked about the colours and patterns to try distracting him from the noise. It sort of worked in that he did start replying to me, still clinging. I was proud of the way he handled it, actually. It would've been so easy for his behaviour to have deteriorated.

As we left, we had a conversation:

>**Me:** What did you think, Munchkin? Did you like the procession?
>
>**Munchkin:** Yes, it was good, but I didn't like the fireworks. They were too noisy.
>
>**Me:** They are noisy, aren't they? I like the colours and patterns they make though.

Munchkin: Hmm. Why do they put someone on the bonfire?

Me: It's not a real person, just a pretend one they make. It's part of the tradition of bonfire night that they burn a person they don't like. It is a bit odd though, isn't it?

Munchkin: Yes. It's not nice to burn people.

Me: No, it's not.

Munchkin [as we walk past a chip van]: Can I have some chips?

I do love the way they suddenly start focusing on something else!

Day 221

Munchkin had been attending Beavers for a few weeks, but not enjoying it one bit. He'd gone because it was something he'd done before he moved in with me and he'd wanted to carry on. With his birthday just gone, he was ready to move up to Cubs, which he did, though not without nerves.

The Cubs leaders were brilliant and settled him in over several months. All of the leaders were great with him and helped when he was having a cling-on moment. He continues to go now and has learnt to love it… most of the time. He doesn't *always* want to go, but I've adapted to know when to make him and when to let him stay home. When I do push him to go, he will often come out and thank me for making him, so I know I've made the right choice.

They do some brilliant activities and I've witnessed it helping his confidence no end. I help out there too sometimes, which is something I never thought I would do! Munchkin has told me how much he loves it when I join in, as he enjoys us being together. Me being there seems to help him relax and feel safe, which is beneficial as he finds it so hard. Engaging in the activities he does is another way for us to bond. And I'm getting used to assisting in the activities. Gradually!

Day 242

When Munchkin first moved in, it didn't take long before we started having tickle fights. He is ticklish – very ticklish – as am I. It was a fun way to create a bond. After a while, it became clear that the tickle fights sometimes caused him to completely de-regulate (unable to manage his emotions in the moment) and he'd end up getting cross, sometimes violent. On the advice of the therapist we'd been seeing earlier in the year, I stopped for a while, before re-introducing much shorter tickle fights.

On this day, Day 242, Munchkin had been angry about something. I don't even remember what is was now, but I pulled him towards me to hold him and give him a hug. It helps him to feel safe and secure when I do this, which in turn helps him reduce the violence and regulate himself. For some reason, I started to tickle him. Initially, he resisted laughing until he couldn't hold it any longer. As he burst out laughing, he asked me to stop.

Munchkin [through the laughter]: *Stop, stop!*

Me: *Have the grumpies gone?*

Munchkin [still laughing]: *Yes, yes, no.*

Me: *I'll have to keep tickling then, until they're all gone.*

Munchkin: *No, no, they've gone. I promise.*

Me: *Okay, if you're sure?*

Munchkin: *Yes, yes!*

He was absolutely fine after that. Meltdown averted. Since that day I've often tickled the grumpies out of him or used humour as a distraction, just enough to steer our way around a meltdown where I could. After all, laughing makes us all happier.

Days 275 and 276

Munchkin was desperate to decorate the house for Christmas, something I've never done before, because I'm not usually home around this time of year. Before Munchkin was in my life, I always went away.

I didn't want a tree with a kitten in the house. It's bad enough with cats, but Timmy the Tabby was a climber, and I could see the tree being bereft of baubles quick smart. That's assuming it stayed standing! Anyway, I was 'persuaded' (you know the way children do), so we went out to buy one. Munchkin was excited at getting a real tree and being able to choose it himself, albeit with some subtle – well, not *that* subtle – guidance. We bought extra decorations to hang around the house. For once, I actually enjoyed it and you could almost say I got in the Christmas spirit, shocking a fair few people I know!

This was the first year I'd spent Christmas in the UK for several years, as I'd been going to see my parents each year while they were abroad. Where they'd been living overseas, it was beach weather at Christmas and this sun-lover couldn't resist a nice warm holiday in the depths of our winter. My parents were back now though, so we decided we'd all go there for Christmas Day. I wasn't sure how Munchkin would cope with Christmas and for that reason I didn't want us to be home alone. I imagined he'd be better in amongst the family, as he was used to busy family Christmases with his foster carers. We'd stayed at my parents a couple of times, so it wasn't new to him, and he seemed okay with it when I told him. If he hadn't been, his behaviour would have shown that pretty quickly, I'm sure.

I'm not one for the commerciality of Christmas and I don't go overboard with presents. As a family, we tend to only get each other a small gift each year. This year, though, I told my parents to decorate the house, at least a bit. And presents were now called for! I bought a 'Stop here, Santa' sign and some reindeer food. Munchkin was keen to make sure Santa knew where he was going to be, since he wasn't at home. We set out everything, including the carrot, milk and mince pie, then went outside to 'watch Santa fly over'. (It was a space station, but there was a lot of hype about it being Santa.) I managed to persuade him to go to bed at a reasonable hour so that Santa could visit and thankfully he was so tired he fell asleep without too much hassle.

Of course, Santa delivered Munchkin's presents and ate the mince pie. He even left a little letter.

Christmas Day was a *very* early start, as it is for so many families. Bless him, he managed to stay in his room until 6am, before coming to get me and shouting in my ear that Santa had been. Just how I wanted to wake up on Christmas Day! I will never forget watching him open his stocking that morning; his reaction melted my heart. He was giddy. Every time he opened something, he thanked Santa for it, telling me what it was and how he wanted it.

Then we had The Santa Conversation:

> **Munchkin:** How does Santa know where I am?
>
> **Me:** Well, we put the sign out and his elves are very clever. They can see the signs and have special magic to know where all the children are.
>
> **Munchkin:** Really?
>
> **Me [wondering if I should really be lying like this to my eight-year-old]:** Yes, there's lots of magic about Christmas.
>
> **Munchkin:** Hmm, okay. How does he know what I wanted?
>
> **Me:** Well, again, Santa and his elves are very clever and they just know. They also ask the mummies and daddies for ideas.
>
> **Munchkin:** Oh, so did he ask you?

Me: Yes, he did.

Munchkin: That's good and it's good you knew what I'd want. That's because you're a good mummy.

Me [trying not to cry]: Thank you, sweetheart. Happy Christmas.

Phew! Clearly a good enough explanation. He started playing with his toys.

The rest of the day passed well. Our Christmases are always low key, but we kept it deliberately so this year, to help Munchkin cope. We spent the morning playing with his toys, and in the afternoon, went for a walk along the beach and messed around in the sand. It wasn't exactly warm, but super fun all the same.

I knew that the hardest part of the day would be Christmas dinner, which we were having in the evening. The Christmas meal is one of those meals that many of us have a set idea about and Munchkin can be funny with food. He's getting better now, but back then, everything had to be just right and as he expected it. I knew that our Christmas dinner would be different to the picture he had in his mind, so I'd tried to prepare him in advance by talking through what we were having. He has a real love of vegetables (still amazes me the ones he eats) and was expecting certain vegetables with his dinner. He loves sprouts, unlike the rest of us, but there weren't any. This made him upset. Then there was the gravy issue. It was *different*. He wanted some. Then he didn't want some. Then he wanted it *there* on the plate. No, he wanted it *there*. He didn't want it on the potatoes so they had to go on a separate plate. And on it went until eventually we worked it out and he was satisfied. I could feel myself getting frustrated and had to keep reminding myself it was because he was anxious, not doing it on purpose or trying to be difficult. Once we started eating, he was fine and had several helpings.

Next came the Christmas pudding. We got ready to light it, but Munchkin having never seen this before, was a little bewildered by what was going to happen. To feel safer, he sat on my lap to watch. I wish I could have seen his face when my dad lit the pudding. Sitting behind him, all I could see was his wide-open mouth. When it went out, he wanted Grandad to do it again and Grandad obliged. Amazed by it, Munchkin quizzed us and my brother explained why it caught fire. He just has to understand why and how everything happens.

Munchkin stayed up late – probably too late – and overtiredness crept in. Getting him to bed was not easy. With some careful family management, though, we did it. That night was a team effort and I'm so grateful for the help of my family; I'm not sure how I'd have coped by myself.

Boxing Day, as always, was an anti-climax. Usually, I find myself nursing a hangover, although this year it wasn't so bad. Thank God, because Munchkin was in full-on mode all day. Difficult and at times defiant, he'd held it together until then, but couldn't any longer.

Days like this are hard work, particularly when you want to relax. We got through the day with negotiation, bribery and distraction. I'm not one for negotiation or bribery as a rule, but there are times when they work wonders, particularly if it's not me doing them!

Day 286

I started back at work at the beginning of a new school term, so Munchkin was having a return-to-school wobble as I was having a return-to-work wobble. Not great. I'm not sure I helped Munchkin much at the time. Possibly I made him worse with my own anxiety. I have no doubt he picks up on it when I'm like that. Truth be told, I'd never had so long off work and it was hard going back. So much had changed within the organisation, and now being part time, I had relinquished some of my role. Not only that, I had changed as a person; work was no longer my be-all-and-end-all. There was life outside of work these days, and despite the difficulties, I was enjoying being a mum. I'd surprised myself, even, by enjoying being at home, although I knew I was ready to go back.

It didn't take long for my stressful, busy job to start having an effect on me, as I tried to cram my work into two days a week. Despite telling myself I'm superwoman and expecting myself to be, of course I'm not. After a while, it started to show. To be sure I was earning enough, I carried on with some HR consultancy too, so life got busier almost overnight.

Day 301

Our third – and hopefully last – review with the Independent Reviewing Officer (IRO) took place on this day. I knew I wanted to go ahead and start the court process. I just hoped everyone else agreed.

The IRO was due at 9am, but didn't arrived until 10.15am because of traffic. She was due to meet with Munchkin first and chat with him before school. We would then carry on the meeting. As it turned out, everyone else arrived at 10am, by which time Munchkin was starting to get distressed. The IRO arrived and spent 15 minutes with Munchkin by themselves. After that time, I joined them, along with both of our social workers. By the time we got there, Munchkin had told her about our family, who was who, making sure she was introduced to Timmy as the newest member.

He didn't want to leave to go to school as he knew they were all here to talk about our future. Somehow we managed to avoid a meltdown and I took him to school without a problem.

Back in the meeting, we agreed to start the legal process. Such a relief to hear. At that stage, Emily was still required to visit Munchkin on a monthly basis, which he found terribly hard. I managed to get agreement for Mary to do the statutory visits instead, on the grounds that it was less upsetting for Munchkin (and saved his social worker a lot of travel). Having my social worker do the visits seemed to work well. Munchkin was hardly bothered when she came. We had a goodbye meeting with Emily later in the year and he seemed happy with that. It was a nice way to close the chapter.

Day 313

Munchkin had decided he wanted to join the Cubs sleepover and was keen right up until it was about to happen. Before the day came, he'd been looking forward to it and we'd bought him what he needed, much to his excitement. On the day, though, he changed his mind.

Adopting Solo

He wasn't going and that was that. You know, that stubborn, heels-dug-in decision-making children can do? That's where he was at.

Now, I'd got plans to go out for the first time *in months*, so I made a decision of my own. He was *going*! I tried a bit of bribery. For about 30 minutes after me buying him sweets, he decided he would go. Then he changed his mind back again. I got his stuff into the car and managed to cajole him in there as well. When we arrived, getting him out wasn't easy. Then once out, he became a cling-on and wouldn't let go. Again not easy.

Finally, I managed to get him and his stuff (a ridiculous amount for one night!) into the Cub hut where they'd be sleeping. After a lot of tears and hugs, Munchkin let go, and went and joined in. The Cub leader was brilliant and we agreed he could ring me at about 8pm if he wanted to. He did ring and we had a little chat. He said he was okay and had eaten and shared some of his sweets. I said goodnight and off he went.

I went on my much-needed night out with friends and it felt great to go out and relax. I did worry about him, and whether or not I'd done the right thing making him go, but I knew he'd be okay and they'd call if there was a problem. After a rather divine lie-in the following morning, I went to collect him. He was subdued, but said he'd kind of enjoyed himself. I made sure I was there early so he didn't have to worry about me not arriving to collect him. I didn't ask too many questions about what they'd done as he didn't seem to want to talk. He did however enthusiastically tell me how little sleep he'd got because they stayed up late and got up early!

We spent the day curled up together on the sofa watching TV, as he fought to stay awake. I put his quietness down to exhaustion. Throughout the day, he opened up and told me little bits about the camp. It sounded fun after all, even though he was finding it hard to acknowledge.

Day 316

Munchkin was still being violent. I was still being kicked, punched, slapped and more. The reward chart had worked to a point, but not stopped the behaviour entirely. Over time, the aggression had crept back in. While it was decreasing in frequency, violent episodes still happened three or four times a week to some degree.

My social worker Mary had suggested a course about Non-Violent Resistance (NVR) that was supposed to be good for managing violent children. I'd never heard about it but was willing to try *anything* that would help. Despite improvements, I still worried about the future and what would happen if Munchkin continued like this when he was older. His strength was astounding; I knew I wouldn't be able to handle him when he was a teenager.

I went to the course without any idea about what I would learn, or even if it would be helpful. Up until now, no-one had been able to help, so to be honest, I wasn't holding out much hope. When I arrived, it became apparent that the room was full of parents and carers in exactly the same situation as me. Many were in much worse situations and not getting any help at all. In some ways, I felt better knowing it wasn't just me; other parents were going through the same ordeal. It also made me realise that I had to deal with it now and not let it carry on. The fear on the faces of those with teenagers was clear to see.

As we went through the day, the information being shared started to drop into place and make sense. It also seemed logical to me and a better way of parenting a child who has experienced trauma. In fact, it seemed like a great way to parent full stop. Non-Violent Resistance can seem counterintuitive but I've seen first-hand how it works. It is based on the premise that, as parents, if we change our behaviour towards our children, our children will change their behaviour towards us over time. NVR helps us, as parents, to build, or re-build strong relationships with our children and create happier, safer and calmer families. The philosophy itself can be used in many different ways depending on the needs of the family and I started by using two of the pillars, reconciliation gestures and parental presence, which were effective for us.

Reconciliation gestures are where you show your child you love them unconditionally irrespective of their behaviour. This is not the same as rewarding bad behaviour. Parental presence is where you change the type of presence you have with your child so that they have a positive image of you and remember you even when you aren't with them. It seems obvious but it's surprisingly effective.

During the break, I got to speak to the wonderful Dr Jakobs, who was leading the course and was the person who brought the philosophy to the UK. I received some personal help and advice, and found his manner most calming and reassuring.

That was the day things started to change for us. I'll never forget it. I came away with a belief that I could alter the way I was parenting to have a positive effect on Munchkin and stop the violence. I started to implement the strategies I'd come away with straight away and it made a difference immediately. The violence decreased. Don't get me wrong, it wasn't perfect; like all things, it was a few steps forward, a few steps back. Yet overall, we were moving in the right direction and I could see how good Non-Violent Resistance was.

Days 331 to 336

I took time off over half-term and we spent the week together. The holiday started off with Munchkin going to a friend's birthday party. It was swimming, so I decided to stay and watch, then jumped in for a swim while they ate tea. It gave me some me-time and some exercise. Win-win in my book. Munchkin had a great time and it was wonderful seeing him playing with this friends, totally part of the group, which is not always the case.

We went to stay at my parents' for a few days too. I get a bit of a break when we go there (thank you, Mum and Dad), plus Munchkin gets to see his grandparents. We don't see them every week so these times are important for building a bond between them. I know he enjoys it there too. His behaviour is usually okay when we're there, although he can be difficult if we go out, even if he isn't violent. At times like these, his anxiety can kick in and that brings on the hard-to-manage defiance. My parents are always supportive, but still, I used to always want to look like I was in control in these situations and felt added pressure of being with them.

Discounting near-daily meltdowns, the rest of the week was fairly uneventful And we'd turned a corner with the violence, which was starting to wane.

Day 341

It was about this time I decided to rename Timmy the Kitten to Timmy the Killer, or Killer for short. Until now, he'd brought home a couple of 'gifts' (thank God, nothing major). Killer must have been honing his skills and wanting to show us how good he was. Over a few days, we had a whole collection of live/half-live/dead creatures bought home, including a magpie, and what I *think* had once been a mouse. If we were lucky, they were left on the kitchen floor. If we were unlucky, they were chased around the downstairs of our house until I managed to get him, and the creature, out. Munchkin hated it when Timmy brought anything in and always locked himself away somewhere until I'd dealt with it. The amusing part is that's exactly what I used to do; I'd have to ring a neighbour to come and rescue me!

Day 341 was the third day of the 'gifting' spree. So far that morning, Killer had brought me three gifts. I was starting to get frustrated, when I overheard Munchkin telling off the cat. It led to us having this conversation:

> **Munchkin:** He's really naughty, Mum. Do you think we should get rid of him?
>
> **Me:** He is being a bit naughty, but he thinks he's bringing us presents. Do you think we should get rid of him?

Munchkin: Yes, because he's being naughty.

Me: So because he's being naughty, you don't think he should stay? Where should he go?

Munchkin: Back to the rescue centre and they can find him another home.

Me: How do you think he would feel if he did that?

Munchkin: Hmm... he's being naughty though.

Me: I'm wondering if he'd be really upset if he was sent away for being naughty. What do you think?

Munchkin: Maybe, but he should be.

Me: Well, I think he should stay here. He's part of the family and he stays whatever his behaviour. We don't send people away because they're a bit naughty, do we?

Munchkin: Hmm... suppose not.

Me: He doesn't mean to be naughty, does he? He doesn't know we'd rather he didn't do it. And it is normal cat behaviour, if a little annoying.

Munchkin: Okay, let's keep him and give him another chance.

Me: Okay, he'll stay forever whatever he does.

I knew from the look on Munchkin's face he had understood the whole conversation and could see that it related to him as well. It reaffirmed what I'd said so many times: *it doesn't matter what you do, you're not going anywhere*. I hoped it would start to sink in soon.

Day 366

It was our second Easter holidays together and a year since Munchkin and I had met for the first time. I couldn't believe how quickly the time had gone. We went away to stay with my friend S and her children again. This time when we arrived, Munchkin jumped out of the car and disappeared inside to play. What a change! It was so lovely to see. We spent a wonderful few days with them, including going to an adventure playground together. The kids had a great time and it was relaxing for me to be able to just sit and chat without worrying about him all the time. It was virtually meltdown-free, which was even better.

On one of the days, we were walking along a river with the intention of feeding the ducks. It didn't occur to me that Munchkin had never done it before, as it was something I'd done all my life. I couldn't understand what was wrong and why he was hanging back. Finally, I got it out of him and he said he was scared. I was proud of him for being able to tell me. I helped him feed them, showing him what to do, with him copying me and laughing. His little face lit up until the ducks decided to get out of the river and swarm around us. At that point he ran away, quickly followed by the ducks. It was quite a sight. And yes, after having a bit of a giggle, I did run over and rescue him.

The whole trip felt like a much-needed break. If only the journey home hadn't been in torrential rain with the motorway starting to flood. Not my idea of fun, but at least Munchkin slept for a large part of it.

Day 376

One year in and it was our first visit to meet some of our extended family. We were visiting an aunt and uncle of mine, who live on a smallholding. It was lambing time and Munchkin was eager to see the lambs.

From experience, caution crept in about how he would cope, and whether we'd have meltdowns while we were there, but I needn't have worried. Munchkin absolutely loved it. As soon as we got there, he was out of the car and went indoors. He relaxed straight away, as if he had been there before. I was totally amazed. I'd shown him lots of photos of where we going and who we were seeing, plus he'd spoken to them on Skype at Christmas, but I didn't think he'd relax quite *this* quickly. He fell head over heels for the lambs and wanted to know *all* about them, including how to look after them. Adorable. He kept climbing into the field to take care of the young animals and adored going into the lambing shed. We even watched one being born. Well, he did. I was looking the other way while making all the right noises!

Getting Munchkin to leave to come home wasn't easy. And I had to check the car for lambs, just in case! Then again, I hate leaving the smallholding as well, so I understood how he felt.

Since the weekend passed so beautifully and without any meltdowns, it showed me how much he loves being outside and around animals. Since, I've made a big effort to do outdoorsy activities whenever we can. Sometimes it's hard to get him there, of course. (Cue: full-blown meltdown.) Yet once he's out, he loves it. He's even worked out where he'd like to buy a farm and what animals he wants. ('*Not cows. They don't make you any money, Mummy*' – heaven knows where he's got that from, though it's true!)

Day 406

Over a year in, I started realising how isolated I felt as a single adoptive parent. I felt like I wanted to extend my support network to other parents who understood what I was going through. I started searching around for support groups and forums. The problem was going out in the evening was near enough impossible and daytime groups clashed with my work days.

And so, I went on a mission. I contacted some other single adopters through various forums and spoke to them about how they felt. I wanted to know what, if any, support they felt they needed. From those conversations, a little idea sparked in my brain and a few months later I set up the Single Adopters Network, which is how I now connect with other single adopters. Why single adopters specifically? I know there are lots of similarities between us and couples who adopt, but there are also lots of differences. Sometimes you just want to talk to someone who has walked in your shoes.

The network has helped me immeasurably since it started and I hope it's helped others as well. Sometimes helping others is the best way to help yourself. Knowing you're not the only one in a particular situation is so beneficial.

Day 416

Up to Day 415, Munchkin and I had only been apart overnight when he'd gone to camp with Cubs for about 15 hours. This was the first time I was going away and we wouldn't see each other for more than a day. My wonderful brother agreed with a little arm-twisting to look after Munchkin. He was at school so it was 'only' after school, the following morning and then after school until I got back. I was lucky enough to be going to Paris, business not pleasure. I'd never been there and would have the opportunity to look around a little during the trip. I was thrilled to be going. It was a city I wanted to see and the thought of a night away in a hotel was blissful. I knew I wouldn't have long there or much time to see the sights, but I miss walking around cities and experiencing other cultures.

I had a few hours to myself first thing in the morning and had a real sense of freedom for the first time since becoming a parent. I only had to think about me, no-one else. It was heaven. At the same time, I was worried about leaving Munchkin. I knew he'd be okay, but it was still hard not to worry. So I spent 24 hours away from home in a beautiful city with a real mix of emotions.

I rang Munchkin when I arrived in Paris that evening (thankful for the time difference) and then again in the morning. I could tell he sounded anxious, even over the phone, but also loving time with his uncle, who was great at playing Minecraft, unlike his mother who refuses to play. When I got home, he was sound asleep on the sofa, having refused to go to bed until I got home. The report was optimistic: he seemed to enjoy himself. And I have to say having a night away did me the world of good.

Day 441

After using Non-Violent Resistance for several months since the course, I was seeing a significant improvement in my relationship with Munchkin and his behaviour. I'd adjusted the way I parented and reacted to situations to bring about the change, instead of trying to force Munchkin to change. I had read everything I could find that made sense from a parent's perspective (there's a lack of literature for the parents) and tried to implement it. I decided I wanted to learn more though, so enrolled on a longer course with Dr Jakobs for a few months' time. My excitement was building about how this could change everything for us as a family.

I talked to my social worker about it, mentioning the impact it had had. If it could work for me, I believed it could work for anyone. One of the main differences I could see was how much more settled Munchkin was. It was easier to get him to school in the morning. He got himself up and dressed, ate breakfast and managed to get into the car without resisting anywhere near as much. It wasn't perfect, just better. That change alone – more successful meltdown-free mornings – made it worth using NVR. Mornings became far less stressful, and not being a morning person, that was seriously great for me.

Subtly and slowly, though, other changes started to appear. Often, it took other people to mention them before I noticed. Munchkin appeared a bit more confident around other people and relaxed slightly more quickly. Again, not perfect but improving. Finally – finally – I felt like I was getting somewhere.

Day 476

I have family down in Cornwall and decided it would be nice for Munchkin and me to go stay. They live on a farm and life is pretty relaxed. After a long drive, we arrived to be greeted by three big bouncy dogs. Slightly hesitantly, Munchkin got out of the car, but his hesitation faded when, a few seconds later, he realised the worse that would happen would be being licked to death!

While we were down in Cornwall, we spent time playing on the beach. Munchkin loved being in the sea, but I'm not such a fan, so stood and watched from the safety of ankle depth, ready to charge in if needed! We had parked ourselves by mussel-covered rocks and obligatory rockpools, neither of which Munchkin had seen before, so we spent time looking for what we could see. We talked about how the rockpools formed and how the mussels lived. We dug deep holes in the sand and buried our feet, played bat and ball, and had fun together. It was one of those days I'll remember for a long time, seeing Munchkin so enthusiastic and playful.

The following day was the village fair, which my aunt and uncle were organising. Somewhat typically for England, it decided to rain hard all day and had to be moved inside. As part of the fair, there was a dog show and Munchkin wanted to show my uncle's dog. In the end, he showed all three of them and won four rosettes. He was so very proud of himself, as was I. The competition wasn't exactly fierce with only three other competitors. Plus, there *may* have been some bias. But nonetheless, I had one smiling child, showing his rosettes to anyone who would look. What more can a mother ask for?

Day 486

On the four-hundred and eighty-sixth day into our life as a family, the Adoption Order was granted.

After a few false starts from clerical errors and me having my heart in my mouth all morning, I got the call. It was all official and legal. Munchkin was fully adopted. It was such a relief I burst into tears. No more regular reporting to Social Services. No more explanations. No more seeing his birth name pop up on the screens at the doctors. Munchkin would take my surname, which would make life a lot easier.

When I picked Munchkin up from holiday club, I told him the news. From his reaction, I couldn't really tell how he was feeling. A mixture of happiness and sadness, perhaps. Later that day, he said he was pleased it was all official. But then at bedtime said he wanted it all cancelled and that he didn't want to be adopted. I guess it was hard for him to cope with. He knew he was now officially cut off from his birth parents and I was aware of how much that worried and upset him. It continues to now. I understand where his worry came from in that respect, but I can find it hard to hear at times too.

Day 501

I enjoy horse-racing (and the people-watching that goes with it!) and introduced Munchkin to it the year before. Since he enjoyed it the first time, we've been a few times and always had fun. It can get quite crowded, but remarkably that doesn't seem to bother him. He likes to stand right on the rail and watch the horses come down the track, shouting loudly for the one he wants to win. Usually, we go with my parents and get all dressed up, Munchkin adorable in his handsome little suit.

We went again on Day 501. This particular day, he had jeans on with his shirt, a tie, jacket and pair of sunglasses. I was persuaded to take countless photographs of him in 'cool' poses, once he realised he looked rather good! I have to admit he did. So much fun.

I realised over the course of the day that Munchkin is *surprisingly* good at picking the winner, or at least a horse that comes top three. I like to have a little flutter at the races and have started taking his advice, rather than relying on my own instinct, as his is definitely better. We watch the horses in the parade ring and he decides which he thinks will win. I tend to choose the jockey with the nicest bum, or the horse that looks prettiest. (Yes, I am *that* scientific!) However, I do sort of marry that information to the horse's form. My son, though, won't tell me what system he uses and now likes to place a bet himself. Obviously not literally. He does regularly come out on top though – slightly annoyingly, because that's all I hear about for a few days thereafter!

Day 505

We got home that evening and I collected the post from the front doormat.

Now, there's something you should know about one of our cats. She had recently taken to going to the toilet just inside the front door. When I picked up the post that day, I saw the cat had managed to poop on some of the post. As I carefully opened the envelope, I realised that that the one she'd pooped on was the one containing Munchkin's new birth certificate. I found it quite funny and Munchkin asked why I was laughing. When I told him, he said, 'Oh right, that's what she thinks of me being adopted!' He went off to find her, gave her a hug and said 'Sorry, you're stuck with me'. It was so cute to see. At least he could see the funny side.

Day 511

On this day, I started the Non-Violent Resistance training. It was the first of a four-day course and I went not really knowing what to expect. It turned out I was the only parent in the room; everyone else was there in a professional capacity. To start with, that made it a bit overwhelming, but the information started to sink in. As it did, I realised just how much sense it made. I knew it worked from the little I'd already learnt from the earlier course and the reading I'd done, but this was at a much deeper level.

I reached the conclusion that I'd found a way to parent that felt right and totally in alignment with my own thoughts. I came away from the first day with new ideas, a real sense of positivity and an uplifted feeling. On the train home, I sat and wrote in my journal all of the thoughts going through my head. I didn't think about how it sounded; it was a stream of consciousness with the words just falling onto the page. It's amazingly therapeutic to write like this. For me, it helps my brain sort out all the thoughts I'd been having and the information I'd received that day.

All four days of training were amazing and literally life-changing. I've implemented everything I learnt and it has made such a difference. It has left me feeling much more confident in how I'm parenting. What I love about NVR is that it's about action, not words, which is something I can do. It's also not a rigid process. You use the framework and principles as a basis, adjusting them for your own situation. It doesn't matter if you get it wrong – that's crucial to remember. Before I had felt like getting it wrong meant I'd failed as a parent. With NVR, it's different. I can't get it 'wrong' because of the way it works. I can just do it better. And if I don't do it as well as I would like or do something I feel is 'wrong', then I can apologise and carry on without feeling like I have to start all over again. I've definitely slipped off the ladder a few times, but it's easy to get back on. Usually I'll apologise, do some sort of reconciliation gesture and carry on.

I've explained to Munchkin about NVR and why I did the course, which I think helped allay some of his anxiety. He likes to know where I am each day and what I'm doing. I've no doubt some of that is wanting to feel in control. Telling him about the course was natural as it was just part of my day.

Day 531

Today was our Celebration Day in court. To be honest, I was expecting a meltdown at some point that morning, triggered by the fear of going somewhere new, not wanting to leave the house, or some random problem I couldn't predict or control. To my utter surprise and joy, though, we were completely meltdown-free. It wasn't a long affair, 20 minutes or so, but done in a way that felt celebratory; it made the adoption feel real. As the judge was talking, I felt myself well up and had to fight back the tears. I didn't want Munchkin thinking I was unhappy.

Munchkin got to sit in the judge's chair and we took photos. It was just us, my parents and my social worker. Afterwards Munchkin, Mum, Dad, Mary and I went out to a coffee shop to celebrate. Munchkin went into school in the afternoon and wanted to celebrate with his class too, so he took in a load of sweets and cakes. He had taken pre-orders so I had strict instructions on what to buy! His Learning Mentor went into the class with him and explained what had happened that morning. Apparently, all the class clapped when they heard the news. Even now, the thought of them celebrating with him fills me with joy.

In the morning, the judge had prompted a conversation that went like this:

Judge: Do you know why judges wear wigs?

Munchkin: No.

Judge: It's because we are all bald.

Munchkin: Really?

Judge: Yes.

Well, as you can imagine, that spiralled off into questions about whether lady judges are also bald. I said he'd have to ask one if he ever meets one. He regaled this conversation to the class, and I had to have several conversations with other mums in the school, whose kids were all convinced judges are bald!

Day 538

Our relationship and life at home seemed to improve hugely at this point. It was less stressful for me and Munchkin seemed happier and more relaxed on the whole. The meltdowns became less frequent and shorter lived. I have no doubt the NVR was making a significant impact, as I managed situations differently.

I reacted and responded in softer ways that he wasn't expecting, using the various NVR techniques. I tried hard to not let his behaviour affect how I felt or acted. I was spending more time each day fully engaged with him, rather than playing or chatting with my mind elsewhere.

Munchkin told me for the first time that day how much he enjoyed and still enjoys those times we spend together. It's a day I'll remember when he said that, albeit with a pang of guilt that I maybe hadn't done enough of this kind of engagement before now. I think going to court helped settle him more too, because at last Munchkin knew for sure he wasn't going anywhere. The judge had confirmed it. He was officially a Fisher and that meant a lot to him. He had his own forever family.

Day 543

Munchkin's school have a Harvest Festival service every year in a local church. Each class has a turn on stage and it's usually a nice child-led service. The first year that Munchkin did it, he didn't want to go on stage, then complained to me afterwards because he wasn't at the front. I didn't quite know how to respond to that one. This year, he had a solo speaking part and was a mixture of nerves and excitement. That's not always the best combination for Munchkin, let's be frank! Yet with some tactful manoeuvring, I managed to avoid a meltdown. Instead, he just bounced around all over the place for several hours until I delivered him to the church and his teacher.

I went into church and managed to get a seat where he would easily be able to see me. When it came to his class's turn, he walked on stage and spotted me. His little face lit up and went bright red with embarrassment at the same time. It was a picture. As they each said their line, the microphone was passed along the row. When it came to Munchkin's turn, he was word-perfect and he beamed afterwards. My heart swelled with pride watching as this small, shy, nervous boy managed to stand on stage and shine. I picked him up from school in the afternoon and said congratulations. He hardly acknowledged me, then changed the subject! He didn't want to talk about it, although I did see a teeny tiny smile creep across his face. He finds it hard to accept any form of praise and will always bat it off. It's moments like this that make it all worthwhile.

Day 551

There was less anxiety about his birthday this year as he'd had one with me already, so knew what to expect. He had a roller-skating party, which I'm pretty sure I enjoyed as much as he did. I can skate (sort of!) and Munchkin spent at least half of the party clinging to the side until he built up the courage and skill to come into the middle. Again, I was glad to see him getting on well with his friends and having a great time.

At Munchkin's request, we had a family party and went out for a meal too, where he enjoyed being the centre of attention. The restaurant staff brought him a balloon and sang happy birthday when they served his ice-cream with a candle in it. It made his evening!

As usual, he'd written an exceedingly long present wishlist and I managed to buy something on there that he still wanted. The list had a habit of changing regularly, so I had to hope he didn't change it again after I'd bought the present. The look of upset isn't worth it, although I do believe that we should be grateful for any gift we receive, whether we are an adult or a child.

Day 571

It was half-term and I spent the first two days attending another NVR training. Munchkin spent one day with my mum and another with the childminder, having a great time. I don't think he even noticed I wasn't there and again I gained so much from the training. Win-win. Being in a room of people who understand and want to support parents is an experience I can recommend. Our focus was on child-on-parent violence and that isn't an easy subject, but I came away feeling uplifted and energised.

We spent the last few days of half-term together having fun. We went to the park, saw friends and played at home. By the end of the holiday, it's safe to say I was ready to go back to work for a break! I love my son dearly, but I'm also a bit of an introvert, so need my own space – something I don't get enough of during the holidays.

On this particular day, we were going to the opticians for Munchkin to have his eyes tested. He is supposed to wear glasses, but rarely does, despite having some pretty cool specs. The optician hadn't read Munchkin's notes before the appointment and read them aloud in front of us. Unfortunately, he assumed that where it said 'mum', it meant me, but in that case, it didn't. That certainly caused an awkward moment. It wasn't his fault, but it was an event that made me realise I needed to ask organisations we deal with to make his notes clearer. Luckily, Munchkin didn't seem to mind.

Afterwards, he chose some new glasses, because he thought he might wear them more often if he got new ones – it doesn't appear to have made any difference from where I'm sitting! This is where his inability to make a decision comes to the fore. After a while, I started to feel sorry for the woman helping us, although she was outwardly brilliant. Finally, after trying on nearly every pair they had, Munchkin narrowed it down to half the options. We were making progress. He chose two pairs, but then wanted them to go dark in the sunlight, like mine do. There was a long-ish discussion about why he wasn't having lenses like that. He was a bit grumpy, because apparently that's unfair, but a trip to his favourite coffee shop seemed to help with the injustice of it all!

We managed to leave the opticians eventually and I collapsed on the chair in the coffee shop, while Munchkin talked about how he had decided which glasses to buy. I honestly didn't think someone could talk that long on a subject like glasses, but I was proved very wrong! On the plus side, I was only required to nod occasionally, so I sat thinking about other stuff I had to do and day-dreaming.

Day 591

It was the annual fair at Munchkin's school and I was part of the team organising it. It meant a long day on site and lots of hanging around beforehand for Munchkin. He was amazing though, hardly complaining, and I gave him several jobs to keep him occupied. He likes having things to do, rather than being left to his own devices.

That day, I'd arranged for him to see Santa and given him some money to spend, because he loves buying gifts for people and wanted to get some of his Christmas presents. His choices of presents are usually spot on; he had a real knack for getting what people wanted. Lots of his friends were there and he spent most of the day playing with them and eating what I suspect was a lot of sweets! My wonderful mum turned up at lunchtime to look after him and then take him home while I cleared up. Munchkin proudly showed her round the fair and then went home with her to play Minecraft. (I'm so glad Mum has the patience to play that!) After all the activity, Munchkin was unsettled in the evening, but otherwise not too bad.

Day 611

On our way into town, we go past a pottery studio, the sort you can go into and paint a piece to bring home. I've always avoided it, partly because I assumed it would be expensive and I wasn't sure it was something Munchkin would enjoy. I could see him going in and not be able to choose something, then having a meltdown, which I wanted to avoid.

Munchkin, however, was keen to go and kept asking me. After a good six months, I caved and decided we would give it a go. The day we went, he was calm and his behaviour had been settled, despite Christmas coming up. In we went to decide what we'd decorate. I suggested we chose something small to start and he agreed. He picked a jug, just like I did. One of the staff showed us what to do, and Munchkin watched and listened intently before getting started. We were painting away, when I noticed out of the corner of my eye his choice of colours... Hmmm... I'm a bit of a perfectionist when it comes to such matters and always want it to 'look right'. I'm no expert, but I was trying my best to colour co-ordinate *my* jug with my kitchen. (Yes, I'm *that* person!) I bit my lip and praised Munchkin for what he was doing. I could see he had a plan in his head and was working away quietly. It was an interesting combination but he was pleased with it, so I let it go. When we finished, we took our painted pottery to the desk to leave it there and collect after Christmas.

When we went back in the New Year, I was pleasantly surprised. I liked mine and was rather happy with how it had turned out, but it was Munchkin's that made me proud. I hadn't seen the design properly when he'd been painting, but now it was dry, it looked great. He was obviously pleased with it as well and showed it off to my parents when we video-called them later on.

That day, my concerns about mismatched pottery were gladly unfounded. Since then, we've been back several times and I've bought us memberships to make it cheaper. I'm so glad we've found something like this that we can do together whatever the weather, although I suspect I could end up with quite a collection of pottery!

Day 621

Our second Christmas together was as wonderful as our first and slightly more chilled out. I got even more into the Christmas spirit and we'd bought a few more decorations to put up around the house. We bought a tree and positioned it so that the cats couldn't jump into it from any great height. (I'm still finding the odd bauble AKA cat football a few months later, but it pretty much stayed intact.)

Adopting Solo

We spent Christmas at my parents' home again, which meant I had a much-needed rest. I'd made sure Santa knew we were going to be there again – of course – and we left him out a little treat. Apparently, Santa is gluten-free like me. Who knew?!

Christmas morning and I was woken up at the crack of dawn by an excited child desperate to open his stocking. After being dragged out of bed, we crept into the lounge and found it. Of course, Santa *couldn't possibly* leave it in Munchkin's bedroom because he'd start opening them in the middle of the night. Munchkin started to unwrap the presents, seemingly happy with them, if a little confused by some of Santa's choices. It seems Mummy didn't give Santa such perfect ideas this year!

We started building the Lego that Santa had left. Yep, I'm supposed to be awake enough to follow instructions at 6.15am. I can confirm I'm definitely not awake enough. By 7.45am, I was asleep on the sofa and my wonderful parents had taken over. Sounds pathetic, I know. I should have stayed awake, but I was absolutely shattered. Sometimes you don't realise how exhausted you are until you're in a place where you can truly relax. Then your body says, 'Right, sleep time'.

My brother was arriving at lunchtime so I made Munchkin wait until then before opening family presents. It was a little unfair, but he had plenty of new toys to play with from Santa. Bless him, he did manage to wait, although I could tell it was difficult and he kept asking if T was there yet! I got him to sort the presents into piles for each person to keep him occupied and then count how many everyone had. As soon as T walked in the door, Munchkin gave him a hug and starting opening presents. He was so pleased with the gifts he got from us. Then started telling everyone what he had got them and how much it cost! He has a thing about telling people the cost, which I assume is something to do with his past.

The rest of the day went well. We went out to play in the park and had a relaxed time as a family. Dinner time started off with a bit of a problem. There weren't any sprouts again. Personally, I was absolutely fine with that. In fact, I would go as far as saying I was happy about it, but Munchkin was somehow expecting them and got quite upset. I should have thought about that, given we'd had the same issue the year before, but I completely forgot. As a result, Munchkin refused to sit at the table and plonked himself on the sofa in a strop. But it didn't last long. He came and joined us at the table and dinner disappeared surprisingly fast (for him!) given how slowly he eats at times.

Then it came to lighting the Christmas pudding and he wanted to help Grandad this time. I could see this being a disaster, but no! He loved doing it and was still in awe when it caught alight. Thankfully he listened to instructions and stopped when told.

After dinner, my dad brought out a magic trick – a flying saucer attached to him by a tiny thread. Munchkin was enthralled, amazed, confused and excited all at the same time (rarely a great combination). He couldn't understand how it worked and was displeased that Grandad wouldn't show him. He tried to grab it, which nearly broke the thread. His controlling side took over and I had to hold onto him tight to stop him getting overwhelmed. Grandad promised he'd show him how to do it the following day. It took a while to calm him, but he was okay thanks to distraction tactics.

Boxing Day, and Munchkin was up early asking Grandad to show him the trick. Not sure that was quite what my dad had had in mind, but he *did* say the following day. He promised to do it later in the day, so he was pestered until he caved. Munchkin came into the room beaming with pride and showed everyone the trick. It wasn't perfect – a little more practice following the instructions would have helped – but his face said it all.

The rest of the holiday was okay. I use the word 'okay' because it wasn't a disaster but wasn't great either. I was tired and ready for term to start. However, there weren't any major meltdowns so that was a big plus.

Day 631

New Year's Eve had been lovely. I let Munchkin stay up as long as he liked and we'd curled up on the sofa with a picnic – well, a pile of snacks – while we watched TV.

During the evening, we talked about what we'd been doing and started a conversation about what we would like to do over the coming year. I've always reflected on the past year and set my intentions for the following year like this, so I thought it would be a beautiful way to bond if the two of us did it together. We got a piece of paper and started to write down all the things we'd like to do in the next 12 months. It included anything and everything we could think of from days out to holidays. It was great fun and allowed Munchkin to see the future as part of this family even more, which is something I know he worries about. As you can imagine our list was long and somewhat unrealistic – it's unlikely we'll get to Disneyland, Hawaii and Australia all in the same year, but you never know.

Then we picked our top eight from all the ideas and agreed those would go on our vision board for the year. A few days later, we collected together pictures of the places we agreed on and stuck them on a big sheet of paper to make a vision board. That sheet of paper is now on the wall in the kitchen to remind us of what we're hoping to do this year. It's a visual reminder for us and a conversation piece when people come over. I've done vision boards for several years now and they work so well; I'm looking forward to doing them with Munchkin each year.

Day 634

Returning to school unsettled Munchkin. The first day back wasn't easy. He was upset, angry and defiant, but he went into school eventually and was fine once there. At school, he behaves well mostly; they don't see the type of behaviours I experience at home as he manages to hold it all together when he's in that setting.

The following week or so was tough. His behaviour was all over the place, quite unpredictable. He wasn't sleeping well, so we were having broken nights as well. All in all, it was exhausting. After about 10 days, just when I didn't think I could handle much more, it started to improve and he settled again.

Afterwards, I realised that he appeared to have moved to another level of 'settled', seeming more relaxed and happy, as if another worry had been put to bed. I've noticed a pattern where unsettled periods, usually a week or two in length, are followed by Munchkin being a little more confident. It's hard because those periods are full of anxiety, defiance, tears, indecision and pushing me away. Yet having seen this pattern of overall improvement, it makes it easier to get through the difficult patches, knowing there's light at the end of the tunnel.

Day 651

Munchkin went downstairs at 6.30am as usual and immediately shouted at me to come down. I assumed there was another dead animal somewhere in the house, but no, nothing to be seen except Timmy desperate to get under the cabinet in the living room. I ignored it assuming he was after a spider.

We got home that evening and Timmy was still trying to get under the cabinet, so I decided to investigate. That's when I saw the mouse. The poor thing had been there all day and somehow managed to keep safe. Had I realised, I would have shut Timmy out, caught the mouse and released it outside. But no, I went for the silly option – Timmy chasing the mouse around the living room for 20 minutes. Munchkin ran screaming upstairs to his bedroom and shut the door. In his own words, he 'ran off screaming like a girl'.

I opened the front door, blocked off all other exits, and at length, managed to get the cat and mouse out of the house. Munchkin refused to come out of his room until I confirmed it was safe, which I did. Downstairs Munchkin came, only for the cat to run around the side of the house and try entering through the cat flap, the mouse in his mouth. I ran to the cat flap to block it as Munchkin ran back up the stairs. Another 20 minutes later, I allowed the cat back in and proceeded to ground all three animals by locking the cat flap.

I assumed it was the end of it, until a few hours later. I stood up from the sofa and put my foot on something squashy. Thinking I must have dropped chutney on the floor from my dinner, I had a closer inspection and realised it was hair and what looked distinctly like vomited mouse. After nearly vomiting myself, managing not to scream because Munchkin was asleep and cleaning up, Timmy was locked in the living room overnight. He will have had no idea why, but it made me feel better!

I regaled the story the following morning to Munchkin, who found it both hilarious and horrible at the same time. While I love Timmy dearly, he has certainly given us a few interesting times since he moved in.

Day 661

Oh how I love Cub camp! I get a whole 24 hours to myself and don't get woken at 6.30am on a Saturday morning. Bliss. I had a night out with a friend and it was the first time in months that I'd gone out in the evening like a 'normal' person. Two years in a row! It was a little reminder of my pre-motherhood life and it felt fabulous to just be me again. Just to sit and chat in a pub about something – anything – not child-related and have a laugh was a novelty.

The following morning, I was at a parent support group primarily for parents experiencing violence from their children. It focusses on Non-Violent Resistance as an approach to manage and change the situation. It's not an easy morning, listening to what others are experiencing, but having come through the other side of the violence, at least for now and hopefully forever, I can totally relate to how they are feeling and how this work will help them. I came away with a real sense of calm, uplifted in many ways. Often we feel alone in our struggles, but groups like this show we aren't. Others are there to help and support us.

It was this day that I broke the news to Munchkin that he'd be moving schools this coming September. He wasn't particularly happy about it, but agreed to go and have a look at the school. His current school has been brilliant and I know how lucky I have been that they were so supportive. In some ways, moving him is an odd thing to do, given those circumstances, but the smaller classes and better facilities will be good for him. I know he'll be fine once he's there and I have to think about his longer term education. I was expecting a meltdown when I told him, but didn't get one, which says so much about how Munchkin feels more secure. The last time he changed schools, everything changed for him – new mum, new family, new house, the lot. Understandably, Munchkin automatically associated the two when I brought up this school move, so we talked a lot about how the only thing changing this time was school. It's also at a different time of year, which I hope will help make the distinction.

The rest of half-term was lovely. I'd describe it as the best we've had since Munchkin moved in. It was virtually meltdown-free; a couple of small ones at the end of the week, but that was all. Loved it! Munchkin had a cold, so we couldn't do everything we had planned. It was, however, great spending time together, seeing family and friends. There's something comforting about curling up on the sofa together to watch a film in the afternoon, even if you do have to fight to get some popcorn! The recurring conversation we had that week went like this:

> **Me:** Please stop picking your nose.
>
> **Munchkin:** I'm not.
>
> **Me:** Yes, you are. Please stop it. Use a tissue. Here's one.
>
> **Munchkin:** I'm not picking it. I'm scratching it.
>
> **Me:** Oh, I see. So what it is you're eating after you scratch it?
>
> **Munchkin [giggling]:** Bogey.
>
> **Me:** Right, blow your nose and stop picking it, cheeky monkey.

I did think about recording it, so I could just keep pressing play when I needed to; we had it so many times.

When he returned to school, I was saying what a lovely time we'd had, but Munchkin's Learning Mentor came to see me at the end of the week concerned. Apparently, Munchkin's recollection of the holiday was that it hadn't been good because he couldn't go swimming. This made me laugh, but also feel sad. It showed that he still focuses on the negative rather than the positive. I know lots of people do this, but I find it upsetting; you end up missing out on the positives in life.

Day 682

It was one of those weekends when I wasn't feeling great and Munchkin was struggling. By Sunday, it was going downhill fast. The constant nit-picking, answering back, demanding and generally being difficult was hard going. It's not easy at the best of times, but when your head feels like it needs to explode and you feel sick, it's even harder. And of course, it's exaggerated when there's no-one else at home to hand him over to. By the time it came to dinner, I'd had enough. Somehow I'd managed to avoid shouting until this point, although I have no idea how.

I sent my brother a text message: 'All I can say today is f***ing hell. It's one of those days.' Followed swiftly by: 'Sorry, just getting that off my chest.' He responded with, 'That's okay. You can always have a vent! Hope it's going okay.' That was his mistake – asking me how it was going – because he got a long message back confirming it wasn't!

We managed dinner and (thankfully easy) homework just about. Shower time was another story though and I did lose my temper in response to Munchkin screaming. Once he was in the shower, I just sat on my bed and cried, hoping he couldn't hear me. I'd had enough and couldn't cope anymore that day. I just needed to release all the anger, stress and frustration. I felt better afterwards and managed to wipe my eyes when he called me into the bathroom.

He seemed calmer after that; it was as if we had both needed to let off steam. The rest of bedtime was lovely to the point where we played together for a bit, before reading and having a hug. He asked me if I was alright and I told him I wasn't feeling well, to which he responded, 'You should have told me. I could have looked after you.' It made my heart melt when he showed he cared, as it had felt like he didn't all day. Those moments are so precious and it's one that's now in my gratitude journal as a reminder for when I need it.

Day 712

Mothing Sunday is always an interesting day because I know it brings up memories and worries for Munchkin about his birth mum. It's also a day he wants to celebrate with me. This year my parents had come up on the Saturday as Munchkin wanted Grandad to take him shopping. So off they went and I went out with my mum. Munchkin is good at shopping, but not so talented at keeping presents a secret until he gives them. We met back up with them in a restaurant for lunch and his excitement overflowed. He gave me one of the presents he'd bought me. He'd chosen a beautiful pair of earrings, which I genuinely love. For a young boy, he has great taste! He managed to keep the rest of the presents a secret until the following day.

I was woken up early on Mothering Sunday by Munchkin arriving in my bedroom with my breakfast all laid out on a tray. He put it on the side and went down to get something else, so I had time to wake up. When he came back, he gave me the tray before jumping into bed beside me. I had bread, strawberries, yoghurt and Marmite. I managed a couple of strawberries before he ate most of them! I was then given my other presents. A frying pan (slightly odd, but he knew I needed a new one) and a teddy (these are a standard present in our house now). It was a lovely fun day and he was helpful throughout. It left me wishing every day was Mothering Sunday!

Day 733

We spent a few days down at my parents' for Easter and had a fabulous time. Despite the lack of structure, it was meltdown-free and lots of fun. We were outside on the beach, walking, playing in the park, eating chocolate and watching movies when the rain came in. It's two years from when Munchkin first moved in and it's lovely seeing the way he interacts with my parents now. He clearly loves being with them and they feel the same way. Their relationship looks totally natural, as if they've known him his whole life. He's happy staying with them if I go out and now wants to stay over by himself in the next holidays. I'm pleased he feels comfortable and relaxed enough to think about doing that. In practice, it may be very different, but to think about it is an amazing step forward.

My brother, who's much-loved by Munchkin, came down again and got jumped on as soon as he walked in the door. They have fun together and my brother is great at holding the line when needed. Granny and Grandad are getting there, but definitely more likely to spoil him like most grandparents!

Day 741

Two years down the line and our life is completely transformed in so many ways, but there are also many similarities to how we were at the start. We are a family. We know each other well, what makes us happy, what makes us sad. And yet we are also still learning about each other, and ourselves, as we go. I have no doubt that will carry on for good.

Sarah Fisher

There is no violence, at least not at the moment, and there hasn't been for six months. This is a great relief and makes this place a better home to live in. There are still meltdowns, lots of them, but they are much shorter on the whole and I've learnt to manage them better. I'm still far from perfect. Munchkin can push my buttons and make me react in an unhelpful way, but all kids do that, don't they? I don't think we'll ever be completely meltdown-free but the situation is ever improving. He's learning how to manage his emotions, which makes such a difference.

Our relationship is much, much stronger than it was and we have a bond. He comes to me when he's struggling or wants hugs, high-fives and reassurance. He knows I'm there for him. When he's melting down, yes, he pushes me away sometimes, or hides under the duvet. I've been known do to that as well! We are still on the journey and it will go on forever; life is a journey for all of us, and as he grows up, we will face new challenges.

Will life ever be easy as a parent? I doubt it, but then that's not why we get into it. The complexity for me is the other issues my son faces, which I, like so many other parents, have to deal with day in day out. That's the hard, exhausting part that seems to never end, but I love my son and we are a family through thick and thin. I have no doubt the road will be rocky, but we'll travel it together and make sure we have plenty of fun along the way.

I've finally acknowledged that asking for help is a strength not a weakness. I have a fantastic support network around me, a combination of family, friends and Munchkin's school, all of whom are there for Munchkin and myself. I feel lucky.

Adopting Solo

Adopting is the most incredible experience I've ever had. Yes, a difficult, heart-breaking and exhausting one at times. (Quite a lot of times!) But if you can get through the difficult bits, learn that it won't always be perfect, figure out different styles of parenting that work with children who have experienced trauma, you can do it and build a strong bond with your child. In my case, I have the family I wanted – a wonderful loving son, who needs lots of support, love and attention. My life has changed considerably, but it has totally been worth it. I wouldn't change it for the world.

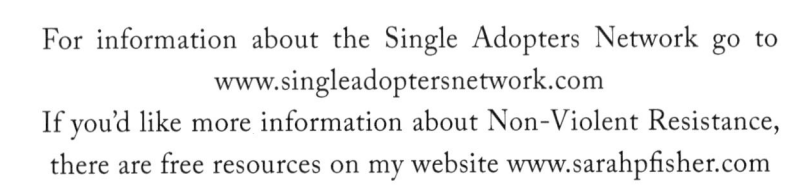

For information about the Single Adopters Network go to www.singleadoptersnetwork.com
If you'd like more information about Non-Violent Resistance, there are free resources on my website www.sarahpfisher.com